THE AYE-AYE AND I

Gerald Durrell

THE AYE-AYE AND I

A RESCUE MISSION
IN MADAGASCAR

Arcade Publishing • New York

First U.S. Edition 1993

Map of Madagascar by TPI

Library of Congress Cataloging-in-Publication Data

Durrell, Gerald Malcolm, 1925–
The aye-aye and I : a rescue mission in Madagascar / Gerald
Durrell. — 1st U.S. ed.
p.   cm.
Includes index.
ISBN 1-55970-204-4
1. Aye-aye — Madagascar.   2. Captive wild animals — Madagascar —
Breeding.   3. Durrell, Gerald Malcolm, 1925– — Journeys —
Madagascar.   4. Wildlife conservation — Madagascar.
QL737.P935D87   1993
639.9′7981 — dc20   92-23211

Published in the United States by Arcade Publishing, Inc., New York
Distributed by Little, Brown and Company

10   9   8   7   6   5   4   3   2   1

PRINTED IN THE UNITED STATES OF AMERICA

MV-NY

Contents

Acknowledgments

All the principal expedition team members join me in offering most grateful thanks to Channel Television Inc. (Jersey, Channel Islands), and the Jersey Wildlife Preservation Trust for providing major funding for the expedition, to Wildlife Preservation Trust International and the Toyota Motor Corporation, each of whom donated a Toyota Land Cruiser, and to Air Mauritius for covering the international air travel for the expedition members, the Channel Television team, the animals and the baggage.

Much appreciation must also be expressed to the Government of Madagascar for granting permission for the expedition, particularly to the Direction des Eaux et Forêts, and to the Director and Staff of the Parc Botanique et Zoologique de Tsimbazaza for the excellent care of the animals before the trip to Jersey.

Without the help, expertise and encouragement so generously provided by many people in Madagascar, the expedition would not have been such a success, and to these people we offer warmest thanks: Roland Albignac, Dennis and Helen Amy, Benjamin Andriamahaja, Mina Andriamasimanana, Alan Hickling, Olivier Langrand, Martin Nicoll, Julien Rabesoa, Mihanta Rakotoarinosy, Georges Rakotonarivo, Raymond Rakotonindrina, Victor-Solo Rakotonirina, Edmond Rakotovao, Guy Ramangason, Joseph Randrianaivoravelona, Celestine Ravaoarinoromanga, Don Reid, Licia Roger, Monsieur and Madame Roland, Eleanor Stirling, Barthélémi Vaohita, Edward and Araminta Whitley, Fran Woods, Lucienne Wilmé and all the people of the village of Antanambaobs, especially Marc and Marlin Marcel.

Finally, we are all indebted to the Channel Television team for their hard work, enthusiasm and good cheer, which made the Mananara leg of the expedition such a memorable experience: "Captain" Bob Evans, Tim Ringsdore, Mickey Tostevin, Graham Tidy, Frank Cvitanovitch and our two brilliant drivers, Tiana and Bruno.

THE AYE-AYE AND I

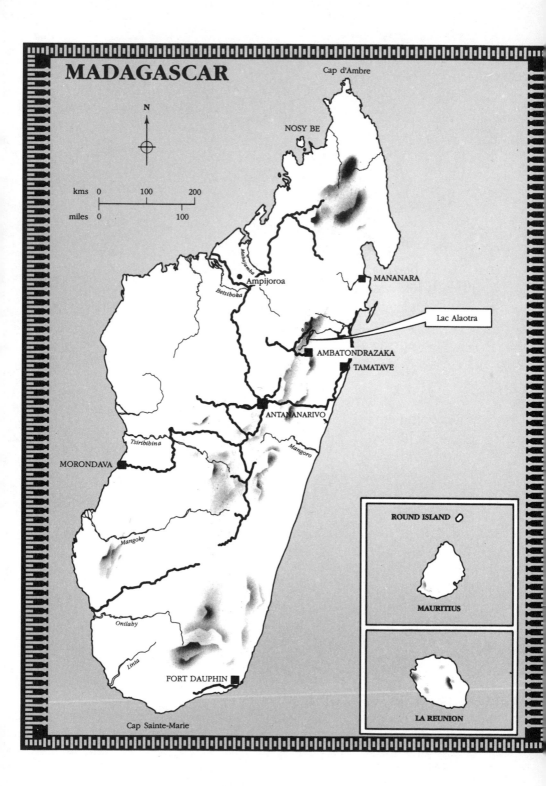

A Word in Advance

In the gloom it came along the branches towards me, its round, hypnotic eyes blazing, its spoon-like ears turning to and fro independently like radar dishes, its white whiskers twitching and moving like sensors; its black hands, with their thin, attenuated fingers, the third seeming prodigiously elongated, tapping delicately on the branches as it moved along, like those of a pianist playing a complicated piece by Chopin. It looked like a Walt Disney witch's black cat with a touch of E.T. thrown in for good measure. If ever a flying saucer came from Mars, you felt that this is what would emerge from it. It was Lewis Carroll's Jabberwocky come to life, wiffling through its tulgey wood.

It lowered itself on to my shoulder, gazed into my face with its huge, hypnotic eyes and ran slender fingers through my beard and hair as gently as any barber. In its underslung jaw, I could see giant chisel-like teeth, teeth which grow constantly, and I sat quite still. It uttered a small, snorting noise like 'humph' and descended to my lap. Here, it inspected my walking-stick. Its black fingers played along its length as if the stick were a flute. Then it leant forward and, with alarming accuracy, almost bisected my stick with two bites from its enormous teeth. To its obvious chagrin, it found no beetle larvae there and so it returned to my shoulder. Again, it combed my beard and hair, gentle as a baby breeze.

Then, to my alarm, it discovered my ear. 'Here' it seemed to say to itself, 'must lurk a beetle larva of royal proportions and of the utmost succulence.' It fondled my ear as a gourmet fondles a menu and then, with great care, it inserted its thin finger. I

1

resigned myself to deafness – move over, Beethoven, I said to myself, here I come. To my astonishment, I could hardly feel the finger as it searched my ear like a radar probe for hidden delicacies. Finding my ear bereft of tasty and fragrant grubs, it uttered another faint 'humph' of annoyance and climbed up into the branches again.

I had had my first encounter with an Aye-aye and I decided that this was one of the most incredible creatures I had ever been privileged to meet. Since it needed help, help it we must. To allow such an astonishing and complex creature to become extinct was as unthinkable as burning a Rembrandt, turning the Sistine Chapel into a disco, or pulling down the Acropolis to make way for a Hilton. Yet the Aye-aye, this strange creature that has attained near-mythical status on the island of Madagascar, *is* in danger of vanishing. It is a magical animal, not only biologically speaking, but in the minds of the Malagasy people amongst whom it lives and, unfortunately, perishes.

When this strange beast was first described in 1782, it had such an anatomical jumble of various qualities that for many years scientists could not make up their minds what it was. Obviously, it was not a common or garden lemur and was thought, for a time, to be a rodent, because of its massive teeth. Finally, it was decided that an Aye-aye was an Aye-aye, one of the lemurs, but a unique inhabitant of the planet, like no other creature. It was dignified with a family of its own and christened with the euphonious name of *Daubentonia madagascariensis*.

Madagascar is an island filled with magic and many taboos, or *fadys* as they are called, which vary from place to place, so it is not surprising that such a weird product of evolution as the Aye-aye should be credited with magical powers that vary from village to village, from tribe to tribe. In places, if it is found near a village, it is thought to be a harbinger of death and so must be killed. If it is a small one, then an infant in the village might die. If it is a large, whitish animal, a pale-skinned adult will be in danger and if it is a dark animal, a dark-complexioned human will be in danger.

In other parts of the island, if a villager finds and kills an Aye-aye near his house, he thoughtfully removes the bad luck from himself by putting the corpse in his neighbour's back garden. The neighbour, finding this somewhat doubtful gift, makes haste to put it in *his* neighbour's back garden. So the Aye-aye corpse progresses through the village until thrown out on to the road to the alarm of passers-by. It is an Aye-aye chain letter: pass this on, or something awful will befall you. In other areas, the animal is killed, its hands and feet bound in raffia and it is hung at the entrance to the village until the corpse starts to rot, when it is fed to the dogs. In other places, its slim third finger is dried and used by the village sorcerer as a magic charm for good or for evil. So the Aye-aye, through a quirk of evolution, has become possessed of a magic finger.

As the Malagasy people continue with their relentless and suicidal policy of 'slash and burn' agriculture, cutting down the forests which are the life-blood of the island, the Aye-aye and many other unique creatures are threatened with extinction. At one time, the Aye-aye was thought to *be* extinct, but then it was found that this curious animal was still clinging on in isolated pockets, nearly all of which were threatened by forest destruction.

The Aye-aye had used its magic to become a survivor of a sort. As its natural habitat diminished, it took to invading what man had replaced it with – coconut plantations, sugar-cane groves and orchards of cloves. With its huge teeth, it trepanned the green coconuts, drank the juice and extracted the jelly-like, unripe fruit by using its thin middle finger like a hook. It disembowelled the sugar cane, leaving the stems looking like some strange, medieval musical instrument. It bisected the clove trees in search of beetle grubs. If you are a villager whose whole livelihood depends on, perhaps, five coconut trees, a tiny patch of sugar cane, and half a dozen clove trees, then the Aye-aye becomes not a magical menace but a creature that can ruin your income for ever. Therefore, you kill it or starve.

As forest decimation continues unabated, these isolated pockets of Aye-aye, leading a bandit-like existence, are doomed. It is to be hoped that new, more intelligent agricultural methods will be soon introduced to replace the destruction. In the meantime, for the sake of the Aye-aye, some must be established in captivity to maintain the species: if they vanish in the wild, we will have at least some animals to return to the natural habitat (if, of course, their natural habitat still exists). At present, there are eight Aye-aye at Duke University's Primate Center in the U.S.A., and one at Vincennes Zoo in Paris. It was essential that more were brought into captivity to build up viable breeding colonies. So the Jersey Wildlife Preservation Trust decided to undertake a rescue expedition to accomplish just that.

This, then, is the tale of our hunt for the beast with the magical finger, and the adventures we had. It is also the story of the Giant Jumping rats and Flat-tailed tortoises of Morandava, and the Gentle lemurs from the reed beds of the vanishing lake. I hope, as well, that it gives a fair portrait of one of the most fascinating islands in the world.

1

The Vanishing Lake

I once described Madagascar as looking like a badly presented omelette, lying in the Indian Ocean off Africa's eastern flank, from which it was wrenched millions of years ago. Like all the best omelettes, well or badly presented, it is stuffed with goodies. The fourth largest island in the world, ninety per cent of its flora and fauna is found nowhere else. Africa is home to one species of pot-bellied baobab tree, Madagascar boasts seven. Madagascar is home to two-thirds of all the world's chameleons, from ones the size of a matchstick to ones almost as long as your arm. And so it goes on, until you become bewildered by the rich biological bounty of the island. It is a treasure trove and, if the mysterious forests are left intact and explored carefully, new and astonishing species are still to be found. Inhabited by wonderful, friendly people, it is a beautiful country, stretching its languid thousand-mile length in blue waters teeming with fish and multicoloured coral reefs. Its forests encompass everything from thick tropical to montane, to dry deciduous forest, to spiny forest as prickly as a hedgehog, and to pygmy forests only six inches high. It has lemurs as big as a four-year-old child and others that are small enough to fit into a coffee cup. It has woodlice the size of golf balls and moths the size of Regency fans. When you go on an expedition such as ours, it behoves you to keep your objectives sternly in mind, lest you be distracted and led astray by the fascinations that envelop you.

The huge island is really a mini-continent of its own, with a climate that varies from wet tropical in the east, to cool

Mediterranean in the highlands, to the baking heat of the desert-like spiny forest in the south. When it was first inhabited by man is still a mystery to the anthropologists: the Malagasy have straight hair and a language which has Malayan-Polynesian similarities. Arguments as to how they appeared in Madagascar are rife. Did they come Kontiki-wise on rafts or boats from the Malaysian region, or did they come land-wise along the coast of Africa? Nobody is sure, but it provides anthropologists with a splendid field for argument and fierce debate, as they pursue evidence as diverse as language, weaving and looms, music and musical instruments, the exhumation of the dead and many other things. It is guessed that Madagascar was first colonized by *Homo sapiens* in AD 500 and, as usual, it spelt doom for the fauna.

Ancestral lemurs were present fifty million years ago and had evolved into many strange forms, including one the size of a calf. There was also the heaviest bird in the world, the gigantic ostrich-like *Aepyornis*, which, it is supposed, was the inspiration for Sinbad's Roc legend, a bird which swooped on elephants and carried them off for food. Although enormous, the *Aepyornis* was incapable of treating elephants in this cavalier fashion – even baby elephants – since, like the ostrich, it could not fly. It is thought that this original faunal bounty, probably as tame as most creatures unfamiliar with man, was ruthlessly hunted and that the clearance of land for crops and pasture destroyed the animals' forest homes. Within a comparatively short space of time, all the giant lemurs and the *Aepyornis* disappeared. In the case of this giant bird, man was particularly shortsighted, for if it had been domesticated, just one of its huge eggs would have provided an omelette *aux fines herbes* for every hut in a largish village.

The Arabs, of course, knew all about Madagascar and, indeed, established settlements in 1300. Then, in 1500, those indefatigable explorers, the Portuguese, under Diego Dias 'found' Madagascar (which had never been lost) on their way to discover a route to the Spice Islands, but Dias' attempt to start a base on the island met with failure. In the fifteenth century, the tribes began to coalesce, first with the emergence of the Sakalava kingdom in the west. In the early sixteenth century, the east of the island was a hot bed of piracy on a grand scale, with all the usual blood-letting, plank-walking and swaggering and where rape and pillage took the form of entertainment. (Now, of course, we can watch it on television.) In spite of this, the peoples of the east were briefly united under a man whose father had been a pirate. The late sixteenth century saw the rise of the Merina kingdom in the central highlands, first under a king whose name, believe it or not, was Andrianampoinimerina, which made lockjaw among his subjects almost inevitable.

Now, the missionaries began to creep in. They had a fairly patchy time, one way and another, under a variety of kings and queens with names as long as comets' tails, until Queen Ranavalona II was baptized in 1869. In 1895, the French established the island as a protectorate and introduced (among many other things) the shaking of hands, kissing on both cheeks and inordinate loquaciousness. A year later, Madagascar became a French colony and, in a typical colonial gesture of gratitude, Queen Ranavalona III was banished to Algiers, where she eventually died. The monarchy was disbanded, but the Queen's remains were returned to Madagascar in 1938.

In 1960 the island achieved full independence. Although the government was anti-West in the 1970s, of late it has displayed a much more lenient attitude to countries who have more wherewithal than the Marxist-Leninist ones.

Antananarivo was looking her best: quaint, red-brick, upright Malagasy houses with wooden balconies standing shoulder to shoulder with modern office blocks in a fine higgledy-piggledy jumble with pot-holed streets running through them. Lac Anosy, the big central lake, was dark as jet and the petals from the hundreds of jacaranda trees planted round its rim provided a blue carpet through which the traffic bustled. Both cars and people were decorated with blue petals as they hurried along the lake's edge. In the distance, huge green trees were spangled with what seemed to be giant white blooms, until one of these 'flowers' took off in slow, graceful flight and you realized the trees held a colony of a thousand pairs of Cattle egrets and Great egrets, the birds taking wing to fly over the city to the rice paddies beyond in search of fish and frogs.

As is usual on any animal-collecting expedition, we were overwhelmed by the contradictory information that well-wishers poured into our bewildered ears, in this case in a mixture of Malagasy, French and a sort of English.

'What are the roads like from point A to point B?' we enquired.

'Mon dieu! Don't even attempt it!' our informant cried, recoiling in horror at the thought. 'Pot-holes the size of wine casks and in places the road completely disappears.'

From other well-wishers, we garnered the knowledge that this same road was as smooth as silk, as rough as a crocodile's back, or just like the Rue de Rivoli, only better.

'What about the ferries?' we enquired hopefully.

'The ferries, you ask? Ma foi, they are never on time and if the tide is wrong you may be held up for twenty-four hours or worse.'

'The ferries? Don't worry, they are excellent, always on time.'

And so it goes on: take rice, don't take rice; take oil, don't take oil; take tinned stuff, don't bother to take tinned stuff. The town of Anamatarateviolala – a name which trips lightly off the tongue – through which we thought we might pass, is described in such glowing terms that we expect to find branches of both Harrods and Fortnum's there. But another confidant will tell you that the town is a gastronomic desert.

'Ask for Pierre,' we were advised. 'He is a mine of information.' And where do we find him. 'Oh, just stop and ask anyone in the street. They all know Pierre, he's the best-known person there. He can fix anything. He could find you a dinosaur on top of the Eiffel Tower, or a deep-freeze at the North Pole.' You begin to long to meet this miracle worker, to lay your head on his honest breast and have all your problems solved. Of course, when you get to Anamatarateviolala you find neither Harrods nor Fortnum's, nor can you find anyone who knows Pierre.

All this takes place in the bar of the Hotel Colbert where several tables have been cobbled together to accommodate your eager well-wishers. The tables are a forest of beer and Coke bottles and the pile of drink tabs is so thick it looks like the proofs of the Gutenberg Bible. In between the bottles are maps, information packs, and frantic notes which later will require a Scotland Yard graphologist to decipher. In front of us passes a kaleidoscope of faces, white, *café au lait*, chocolate, or yellow as chamois leather.

When, finally, we go to bed exhausted, the mosquitoes descend on us, each adding its own piping voice to the insect Mozart opera. The bathwater is dark brown and smells of vanilla. Early morning tea is served by a gentle Malagasy and it is also dark brown and smells of vanilla. I wonder vaguely, as another day dawns, whether they simply fill the teapot from the hot tap in the kitchen. However, an early breakfast of mango, pineapple, lychees and fresh strawberry juice revitalizes the tissues.

In order to avoid the host of informants who are eagerly awaiting our arrival in the bar, we find a back way out of the hotel and go to refresh our spirits by paying a visit to the *zoma*, one of the most fascinating markets in the world.

Here, under the innumerable white umbrellas which, from a distance, make the market look like a field of mushrooms, lies the provender of the city. There were pyramids of pulses, red, green and fawn; twisted bundles of herbs in every shade of green and with strange leaf shapes, looking like fodder enough for a sorceress's stallion; piles of lettuce and watercress, dripping water and gleaming as if newly varnished; a host of powdered spices, like the palette of some Malagasy Titian or Rembrandt, raw umber, rose madder, greens, blues, smouldering reds, and yellows as delicate as a crocus bud, all of them waiting to be mixed with oil so that they could release their many fragrances upon the tongue; bags of beans of bewildering shapes and colours, some round, some like bricks, some as minute as pin heads with what appeared to be neat little black zip fasteners down one side. Next to them were woody chunks of liquorice and vanilla pods, all sharp and tangy to the nose; nearby, pyramids of jade green duck eggs; and alongside these were similar piles of chickens' eggs, white as chalk or brown as toast. Beneath these domes were the chickens, their legs tied together, lying in

9

untidy, indignant bundles like animated feather dusters, and ducks honking gently as they nervously watched the passing forest of brown legs.

Turning from this spectacle we were confronted by huge bowls of tiny fish, glittering like silver coins, and larger ones – black as coal – laid in rows. Next to them lay a panoply of great carp, pouting sulkily side by side, each large scale rimmed with silver or gold so the carp looked as if they were wearing chain mail. Beside them were the meat stalls, the last resting place of the strange, humped zebu cattle, gory carcasses pulsating in a shroud of flies. Nearby was a bowl of skinned and cooked zebu lips, transparent, gelatinous, quivering like dirty frogspawn, with the occasional hair attached. Over the bowl crouched an ancient woman with a face like a walnut, dressed in rags, stuffing these awful slabs into her toothless mouth with the aid of a tin fork. But not far from her could be found stalls covered with beautifully embroidered table cloths and dresses, and vast quantities of brilliant fresh flowers. It was like finding a rainbow in a mortuary. Next to these, tottered piles of raffia baskets like brandy snaps, looking good enough to eat.

Invigorated by the sights and scents and sounds of the *zoma* we made our way back to our hotel room for a conference of war, carefully avoiding the bar full of eager informants bubbling with misinformation.

There were four of us: my wife Lee; myself; lanky, unflappable John Hartley, my PA of many years' standing; and Quentin Bloxam our Curator of Reptiles – tall, muscular, with a determined-looking face that suggested 'Bulldog' Drummond on the way to rescue his wife Phyllis from the clutches of the unspeakable cad Carl Peterson. We sat drinking beer and discussing the *modus operandi* of the trip. We had to go to three places: the Mananara region in the east, where we hoped to catch the elusive Aye-aye, the forests near Morondava in the west, where the Flat-tailed tortoise and the Giant Jumping rat had their respective abodes, and Lac Alaotra, where the Gentle lemur, diminutive and shy, lurked furtively in the reed beds.

We eventually decided to split our forces in order to save time. John and Quentin would take our two Toyota LandCruisers (one

donated by our sister organization, Wildlife Preservation Trust
International, one donated by the munificent Toyota company)
to Morondava and set up camp there. Meanwhile Lee and I
would go north-east to Lac Alaotra and try to find Gentle lemurs.
If successful, we would bring them back and board them at the
Tsimbazaza Zoo in Antananarivo and then fly to join the others
in Morondava. This seemed to us all an excellent campaign plan
and, cheered by our decision, we went downstairs and had a
couple of dozen small, sweet and succulent Malagasy oysters for
lunch to celebrate.

To assist us in our plans for Lac Alaotra, we had enlisted the
aid of Olivier Langrand (who had just published a much-needed
guidebook to the birds of Madagascar) and his beautiful and
formidably capable wife, Lucienne. She had done a lot of work
on the lake trying to track down two species of bird (a pochard
and a grebe), both endemic to the lake and believed to be extinct.
Lucienne told us that it was not possible to work around the
lake without Mihanta. My heart sank. Was this going to be
another of those elusive Pierres who vanished from sight when
you appeared? But no, I had misjudged Lucienne, for the next
morning she appeared, exuding charm and efficiency in equal
quantities, and in tow was a charming Malagasy with a wide,
happy smile and humorous eyes. He was a fourth-year medical
student who had been born in one of the numerous villages
that surround Alaotra and therefore had a sprinkling of cousins,
uncles, aunts, nephews and nieces in nearly every community.
He immediately and deftly took control of our whole enterprise.
We were to fly up to the lake and come back by train with any
animals we obtained. However, he would go ahead by train,
taking our animal cages with him, arrange a room in a *hotely**
and organize transport for us to go and search the villages
around the lake for any Gentle lemur (*Hapalemur griseus alao-
trensis*) kept in captivity. He explained that this was a good time

---

* All restaurants are called by the name *hotely*. As many of them also
have accommodation (of a sort) for the weary traveller, I took to calling both
restaurants and hotels *hotely*s, much to Lee's annoyance, for she is a stickler
about these things. But I stuck to my argument that *hotely* was a far more
enchanting name than any other for such hostelries.

of the year to get lemurs as it was in this season that the local people burnt large patches of the reed beds to make room for more rice paddies. An added advantage was that the lemurs driven out by the flames could be clubbed to death and sold as food or captured and sold as pets. Needless to say, all of this is strictly against the law but continues unabated, nevertheless.

The tale of Lac Alaotra is a dismal one and it is, I am afraid, the sort of thing that is happening throughout Madagascar. To begin with, the lake – the biggest on the island – was Madagascar's rice bowl and met all of the country's considerable needs. (The Malagasy consume more rice *per capita* than any other people.) The lake is surrounded by a picture frame of gentle hills, once covered in forests. However, over the years, these natural bastions that protected the lake were felled for farmland. Thus the forest shield was removed and what was grown on the exposed soil only lasted a few years, after which the hills started gradually to disintegrate. With no trees to hold it in place, the degraded soil made its way down into Alaotra like a red glacier, slowly silting and clogging the waters, slowly making the lake vanish. Now, the lake is no longer the rice bowl of Madagascar and the country has to import this staple food, paying out foreign currency from a feeble economy.

You cannot blame the Malagasy people, but rather the people who have ruled in the past. To the peasant, the felling of a piece of forest is not looked upon as ecological suicide, but as a way of gaining a bit of soil that will give him a crop for a few years, while the forest he fells forms fuel for the fires that feed him. His forefathers did it, why should not he? He does not know that there are five times as many of him as there were in his grandfather's time and that this profligate use of nature's bounty will starve his grandchildren.

Our flight to Ambatondrazaka, the largest town on the shores of Lac Alaotra, was depressing beyond belief. Miles and miles of hill country, once forested, now showed bald and split with a million scarlet wrinkles, the first signs of erosion, the disintegration of the land. The flight lasted three quarters of an hour and beneath us we saw nothing but this horrifying landscape. I said to Lee, 'It's like flying over the Sahara,' to which she replied, 'This is how the Sahara came into being.'

We landed on a grass airstrip and the aircraft taxied round until it was outside the small building that appeared to be control tower, bar and luggage carousel, none of which at the moment were in use. There was no sign of a welcoming Mihanta and again I wondered if he was mythical. We hoiked our luggage outside the air terminal (if you could call it that) and gazed down a long, red-mud road, full of pot-holes and gleaming puddles, for there had obviously been a considerable downpour in the night. The road disappeared into a haze of trees, but nowhere could we see a sign of Mihanta. There was one elderly taxi, into which a very large Malagasy lady, her equally large daughter and a child were being installed.

'Let's get into the centre of town and send out search parties from there,' I said to Lee. 'Let's ask them for a lift.'

With kindly eyes and broad smiles they welcomed us into the cab. There was just enough room. We set off down the road, the car springs squeaking protestations at every pot-hole, the water from the puddles squirting like blood from under our wheels. We had progressed, as on a trampoline, for a quarter of a mile, learning in the course of it all the intimate details of the large lady's private life, when another car approached containing a gesticulating Mihanta. So, in a broken, red looking-glass of puddles, we exchanged cars and compliments, and Mihanta, full of apologies, drove us to our hotely.

By Malagasy standards, this was a substantial building, run by a Chinese man and his Malagasy wife and wonderfully situated on the opposite side of the road to the open-air market of Amba-tondrazaka. I found this fascinating but most distracting. When sitting downstairs in the bar-lounge-restaurant three windows looked out on to the street and the market went on from dawn to dusk.

I noticed immediately that all the women wore hats. Now, I love women in hats, so I was bewitched. Elegant Malagasy ladies would glide past the window, wrapped in multicoloured cloth *lambas* (in which they carried their babies strapped to their backs), peering at you from under the broad brim of beautifully woven straw hats. Of course, the younger ones did not yet have babies. They slid along, their *lambas* wrapped around them to display every provocative curve and, from under their broad-brimmed headgear, they would gaze out with eyes the size of black mulberries. It was an enchanting sight but not, strictly speaking, what I had come for.

Our room was large, full of unnecessary furniture and a bed that must have been designed for St Augustine, to discourage both sex and sleep. Its windows were barred, which gave it a vague flavour of Alcatraz. However, by Malagasy standards it would be rated three stars in the Michelin guide.

The moment we arrived I was smitten with a tummy upset, such as one is prone to in the Tropics. It can either be mild or devastating and painful. In my case it was the latter. Taking vast quantities of medication, I hoped for the best, since Mihanta had informed us that the first thing we had to do was to make ourselves known to the two local presidents – one on each side of the lake – in whose territories we would be operating.

He had engaged a large, handsome Malagasy with the unlikely name of Romulus, who would drive us hither and yon in his battered car, which looked as though it had been salvaged from a junkyard. All the windows were wound down and there were no handles to wind them up. One of the back doors was jammed, both windscreen wipers had disappeared, the front and back of the vehicle had been in close contact at one time or another with a brick wall, the tyres were as bald as vultures and the exhaust pipe drooped behind, making an untuneful scraping noise as we progressed. However, the engine worked, after a fashion, with much wheezing and grunting and occasional gasps and stoppages.

In this decrepit vehicle we made our way to the outskirts of the town to meet the first president. He was a highly intelligent, energetic man and the moment we shook hands with him we realized why he had reached his position. Lee carefully explained our mission to him and he was obviously impressed, not only by Lee's command of French but by her personality. He glanced at me in a friendly fashion once or twice, but for the

14

rest of the time his eyes were riveted on her and he finally said that he would do anything we wanted. I felt that, if asked, he would have happily presented Lac Alaotra to Lee as a gift. We left him in a flurry of good wishes and then drove off to the western shores of the lake to meet the second president.

The drive was depressing. The undulating hills that surrounded the lake were denuded and the flat areas that had once been water and fertile rice paddies were now silted up and sterile. On the scattered weeds that now grew there a few zebu herds and some flocks of geese grazed in a desultory fashion. It was a desolate sight. In the extreme distance we could glimpse the lake and the reed beds, where the lemurs we had come to search for had their ever-diminishing home.

The village of Amparafaravolo was large and fairly prosperous-looking: mud houses thatched with reed and brick-built public buildings. In one of these we were shown into the president's anteroom. Unfortunately, he had been kept at a meeting and could not see us but, we were told, his deputy would see us at two-thirty. By now, the soothing effects of the antibiotics I had taken had worn off. I felt as if I had a very boisterous crocodile embedded in my stomach and the need to be in close proximity to a lavatory became mandatory. So we went to the local hotely and had an uninteresting but adequate lunch.

On the stroke of half-past two we were ushered into the deputy's office. A tall, slender Malagasy with frosty white hair, he was dressed in an impeccable white linen suit, and a gay red and yellow foulard tied round his neck like a bouquet of orchids. The crease on his pants would have brought a flush of delight to M. Guillotine. He listened politely to Lee's description of our quest, but it was obvious that he was more interested in himself than in anything else. He was a bureaucrat who had made it. As Lee talked, outside the window an aggressive cockerel with a harsh crow was telling all the world that this was his territory, and next door someone was attempting to play 'Silent Night' on a piano accordion and coming to grief on the second verse. Our friend in the white suit said he would be delighted to write us a letter which, he implied, would open all doors for us. He then called on his secretary and, while she sat there patiently, he wrote out the letter in longhand and then handed it to her to be typed. She took it away and we could hear her starting to type as if she had only one finger.

By this time, my stomach cramps were extremely painful and the need for a lavatory was paramount. Since it appeared that the letter was going to take as long to procure as the Domesday Book, I requested to be shown the way to what the Americans euphemistically call a 'comfort station'. I was led out to the back of the building – where the harsh-voiced cockerel viewed me with disdain – and then shown towards a breeze-block building approximately the size of a small cupboard. On entering this, I decided immediately that it was the sort of facility even a Greek taverna owner would consider unhygienic. There were two cement footsteps and a hole in the ground. It was the ominous, omnivorous, sibilant rustling noises emanating from this hole that made me realize I was sharing this odoriferous boudoir with twelve million maggots. As well as these companions the place was home to some of the biggest cockroaches I have ever been introduced to. They were considerably longer than my thumb, chocolate and bronze, sliding about silently and gleaming like newly-minted Rolls-Royces. Outside, the person with the piano accordion was still trying to master 'Silent Night' and the aggressive cockerel was accompanying him. Neither could get to grips with the second verse.

I went back to the deputy's office and, finally, the letter was produced. The deputy signed it with a flourish and we all stood up to leave, but then his bureaucratic eye detected a flaw in the document. Our name had been spelt with only one 'r'. So the letter was given back to the abashed and berated secretary to be retyped and we all sat down again. After what seemed like a century, during which the piano-accordion player made no musical progress, the new letter was produced, perused for error, finally signed, and we took our leave. This whole business had taken up an hour and a half of our time and we never had any reason to use the letter.

Meanwhile, Mihanta had discovered by some mysterious means that a cousin of his living in a village some three miles away had a Gentle lemur in her possession and so we drove there to see if this were true. As soon as we got there Mihanta left the car and vanished like a wraith of smoke in that silent, unnerving way the Malagasy have, to reappear triumphantly carrying a raffia bag in which crouched a sub-adult lemur, terrified out of its wits. It transpired that Mihanta's cousin had gone to market that day and had found four or five live lemurs on sale as food items. She had purchased one for the generous sum of seventy-five pence, thinking it might make a suitable casserole for her husband. We reimbursed her the purchase price while explaining that it was illegal to kill, capture or eat these animals – a fact of which she was unaware and which she was astonished to learn.

It was a typical example of an animal being given what I call 'paper protection'. This happens not just in Madagascar but all over the world. A law is passed for the protection of a species but the inhabitants of the country are not told of the law, and there is no money to provide the infrastructure to enforce this law. Thus, to all intents and purposes, the law is useless.

The poor little creature was so scared that I decided not to subject it to further stress by transferring it from the bag to our travelling crate. Lee sat holding the raffia bag on her lap, clasping the mouth of it firmly in case the lemur should make a sudden bid for liberty. I decided that, owing to my somewhat precarious state of health, we should now return to our hotely, where I would have access to some more or less civilized amenities. As we were bowling along in the gloaming, a man suddenly leapt out into the middle of the road and started windmilling his arms at us. Fortunately, one of the few things that did work on Romulus's car were the brakes, but even so this man came closer to death than I would care to be. He informed us that in a village about a quarter of a mile up the road there were three captive lemurs.

Against my better judgement we turned off the highway and bumped and joggled our way down an atrocious road that finally ended in the main square of a quite substantial village. We came to a standstill and I suggested that, owing to her command of

French, Lee should go and look at the lemurs, if indeed there were any, and report back to me. She dumped the raffia bag containing our first prize in my lap and vacated the car together with everyone else. They all simply vanished like assistants in a conjuring trick.

So there I sat, holding closed a raffia bag containing a Gentle lemur on my lap while the car quickly and miraculously became surrounded by some two hundred Malagasy children and a flock of thirty geese. At this point two things happened simultaneously: the lemur woke up and decided to make a dash for freedom and my stomach cramps returned with even more viciousness. I was in urgent need of a quiet place to contemplate what appeared to be my imminent demise. I was also in urgent need of a method of retaining the lemur. If I released my grip on the mouth of the bag the lemur would leap out into the car and, as all the windows were down and there was no method of closing them, it would be out into the countryside in a trice. I could explain my plight to no one, for my audience of two hundred children, who were regarding this strange, bearded *vazaha* (Malagasy for a white person) with the wide-eyed attention that normally one would accord a visitor from Mars, of course only spoke Malagasy, a language not included in my repertoire of tongues. The geese regarded me with interest, honking gently, but were not of any substantial help.

Surrounded by this sea of enchanting black faces, with their astonished black eyes as big as saucers, and an attendant chorus of geese, I reproached myself, as I have done many times, for being so idiotic. As the lemur intensified its efforts to part company with me, and as my stomach cramps grew so bad I felt that someone was operating on my nether regions with a blunt chainsaw, I reviewed my life.

Why, I asked myself, do you do this to yourself? At your age you should know better and stop acting as if you were still twenty-one. Why don't you retire as other men do and take up golf, bowls or soap-carving? Why do you flagellate yourself in this way? Why did you marry a much younger wife who encourages you in these ridiculous acts? Why don't you just commit suicide?

But if I do that, I thought, the lemur will escape. So I came full circle. Pausing at that philosophical point in my meditation, I saw Romulus at the far end of the village street and, without thinking about the effect it might have, I stuck my head out of the car window and yelled, 'Romulus – ici – très vite!'

The children were transformed from immobile, fascinated spectators into a terrified mob. Screaming, they fled in all directions, rushing down alleyways, bursting through doors into the safety of huts, as if the great white Devil Vazaha was after them. The geese, hitherto placid, raised their wings like tombstone angels and, honking like ancient cars in their panic, chased after the children, even rushing into the huts, to be summarily ejected moments later. I have never, in my entire life, effected such a complete and absolute rout on a group of mammals and birds. Romulus came at the run, a look of acute alarm on his face.

'Monsieur,' he said, panting. 'Qu'est-ce que vous désirez?'

'I desire ma femme, tout de suite,' I replied.

He vanished and returned in the space of a few seconds with an alarmed Lee.

'What's the matter?' she asked.

'I cannot cope with acute tummy trouble *and* a recalcitrant lemur at the same time,' I said. 'Let's put it in its bag into the travelling crate. I can't think why we didn't do that in the first place.'

This, and other things, were accomplished, but I fear it will take many years to eradicate from those unfortunate children's minds the picture of the horrifying, roaring, bearded *vazaha*. I am sorry about this, for they deserve better memories of the white races than I, unfortunately, was in a position to give them.

We got back to our hotely and smuggled our lemur in. Over the years I have found that certain hotels object to your keeping a baby wart hog in your room, or fuss because you put snakes in the bath. It is a shortsighted policy which will not bring them custom, in my considered opinion. One is reduced to the vulgar level of a smuggler, having, by subterfuge, to insert a creature into one's room without making the management privy to one's designs. It is a hazardous business. For example, a charming

South American maid once narrowly missed having a cardiac arrest when she discovered that I was sharing my bed not with my wife or mistress (which would have been acceptable) but with a baby Giant anteater.

The lemur, now that we could see him properly, was about the size of a half-grown cat, with bronzy-greenish fur, huge golden eyes and enormous hands and feet. We had stopped briefly on the way back so that Mihanta could collect some succulent reed and some papyrus. Lee mixed this with some chopped carrot and banana. The sooner you can get a newly-caught animal to extend its menu, the easier your task becomes. We could not get that particular species of reed nor, for that matter, papyrus in Jersey, so the sooner we could introduce the creature to such things as bananas and carrots the better it would be. When Lee opened the door of the cage to present the plate of foodstuffs to the animal, it backed into a corner, stood up on its hind legs, eyes blazing, mouth open, arms held wide as if to embrace her.

'There doesn't seem to be anything gentle about *this* lemur,' I remarked as the animal yapped at Lee like an infuriated toy dog.

'Well, you can hardly blame the poor little thing,' said Lee. 'How would *you* feel if you'd narrowly escaped being put in a casserole?'

I had to admit she had a point.

While I sat on our fakir's bed and swallowed quantities of antibiotics aided by quantities of Scotch, Lee went out to the market across the road to see if she could find any more tasty fruit or vegetables to extend the menu available to our new acquisition. The moment silence descended on the room, I heard a scrabbling in the cage, followed by the satisfactory scrunching noises of the lemur feeding. This was a joyous sound, for sometimes a newly-caught animal will suffer a self-inflicted fast for twenty-four hours or longer simply because of stress. If this fast lasts too long, endangering the animal's life, it may have to be released. But an animal which starts feeding at once is more than halfway to reconciling itself to captivity.

Having fed well and noisily, the lemur moved about the cage, exploring, uttering almost inaudible little interrogative mews like a kitten, followed by a long silence. Then, suddenly, it started making the most extraordinary noise that can only be written down as 'yourp'. It sounded like someone pulling a cork out of a small bottle and the first time I heard it I wondered for a moment if Lee, out of the kindness of her heart, had put a small bottle of champagne in the cage with the creature. However, it went on popping corks at regular intervals and I decided that this was a communication signal. In the dense reed beds it is possible that the popping noise carries better than any other sound and this enables the troop to keep in touch without necessarily being visible to each other.

Over the time we had this lemur and others of its kind I was intrigued by their extensive vocabularies, the popping noise, cat-like mews and purrs, yaps like a dog and growls like a mini-tiger. The following morning we found to our delight that our first specimen had eaten all the vegetation we had put into the cage, as well as some carrot and half a banana. When Lee fed him, although he still stood on his hind legs, arms outstretched, mouth open as a warning, he did not yap, which was another good sign.

Mihanta told us that the following day we would be transported by Romulus to the eastern shore of the lake where there was a dense concentration of villages. Here, he was sure, we would find a mate for our lemur and maybe some other specimens as well.

YYYYYYYY

2

 АААААААА

A Flood of Lemurs

The next morning, while I breakfasted on equal parts antibiotics and fried eggs, I people-watched through the restaurant window. Romulus had sent a message to say that his car – not altogether surprisingly – had broken down and that he would be late. This gave me an hour to feast my eyes on the market, which had started at four that morning and was now in full swing. Lee had joined the throng in search of baskets with lids to house any future lemurs we might find, and I enjoyed myself by doing some sketching. As I watched I was able to observe the many purposes for which that item of clothing called the *lamba* can be used.

The *lamba* is a piece of cotton four feet by eight and covered with an intricate and highly-coloured pattern. In my young days, it used to be called a sarong and was worn by Miss Dorothy Lamour, but she used it merely to embellish her manifold attractions. In the market at Ambatondrazaka I saw its uses can be more practical. Firstly, you can wrap it round yourself in order to carry your baby on your back, like a sort of outside womb. If you have no baby you can carry small sacks of rice, or chickens and ducks in the same way or, indeed, transport your lunch in it. It can be used as a dress, a cloak or a hood to keep off the sun, or as a loin cloth. It provides a light, warm cover when you sleep and, last but by no means least, it makes you look pretty.

The Malagasy women are small, delicately boned and walk more gracefully than any ballet dancer I have ever seen, with a magnificent carriage developed from the fact that from infancy they carry things on their heads. Here in Ambatondrazaka with their rainbow-hued *lambas* clinging to all their curves, their dazzling, white straw hats tilted rakishly, they were breathtakingly beautiful. The weights that some of them carried on their heads were astonishing and I wondered how those slender necks could survive without snapping like the stalk of a flower. I saw one lady with a huge basket full of sweet potatoes. It required the help of two of her friends to hoist this burden on to her head and once it was there and settled to her satisfaction she simply walked off down the road as smoothly and effortlessly as a stone gliding on ice. Another lady presented a curious sight, for in the large basket on her head she had two geese. The birds were hidden from the neck down, so it looked as if, in some miraculous way, the basket had sprouted two honking heads.

As I sat in the bar/restaurant a constant stream of people came in with produce to sell to the patron's wife, who acted as bartender. One minute it would be a great tin bowl of fish, the next a covey of squawking upside-down chickens, or else the haunch of a zebu, or a dozen or so eggs. Madame would inspect each offering minutely and either send it through to the kitchen or dismiss the hopeful vendor with a wave of her hand.

While watching this fascinating and colourful pageant, I was joined by Araminta and Edward, friends of ours who had decided to take a holiday and join us, for they are staunch supporters of our work and wanted to see how the collecting was done. Edward's great-uncle, Herbert Whitley, had founded and built the zoological gardens at Paignton in Devon and, in times past, had acquired many specimens from me to add to his collection. He was a wonderful, eccentric naturalist of a sort that only seem to flourish in England and he had a magic touch with all creatures, breeding in his zoo animals that nobody else could even keep alive. Physically, Edward resembled his great-uncle in many ways. He was tall and well-built, with a certain distinctive tilt of the head and a beguiling, innocent, anyone-for-tennis look belied by the determination of his jawline. Araminta, with her smoky, dark good looks and appraising eyes, was a perfect match for her exuberant mate, and I loved the fact that she had been bestowed with such a wonderful Victorian title for, to my regret, some of these lovely old names have gone out of fashion.

On their arrival, jet-lagged and exhausted, two days before, I had greeted them by immediately passing on to Araminta the offspring of whatever bug I was suffering from. She would only forgive me for this unfriendly gesture on condition that I promised to call our first two lemurs Araminta and Edward and, of course, I agreed. Meanwhile, Araminta and I kept going back and forth from the 'comfort station', like the two little figures who pop alternately in and out of those tiny wooden Swiss chalets that you buy to predict the weather.

'How are you today?' I enquired.

'Splendid! Splendid!' said Edward, with all that awful exuberance displayed by the young and healthy at breakfast time. Araminta merely gave me a frigid look.

'What you need is some breakfast,' said Edward, looking at her enquiringly, 'have some chop suey with three or four fried eggs on it. It's delicious.'

'No, thank you,' said Araminta, turning white. 'I'll just have some tea.'

'What's the programme?' asked Edward, engulfing chop suey like one of the larger and less restrained herbivores.

I explained about Romulus's car having broken down.

'Broken down?' said Edward. 'I wonder it goes at all, let alone breaks down.'

'They'll probably be about an hour,' I said. 'So what will you all do?'

'Go Christmas shopping,' said Edward.

'Go Christmas shopping? *Here*?' I said.

'Well, we won't have time when we get back to England, so we thought we'd see what the market had to offer,' explained Araminta.

'They've got some nice chickens and geese,' I said judiciously, 'or did you have pigs in mind? I saw five baby pigs just now, all different colours and about the right size to fit in your rucksack.'

'Thank you, but my thoughts were running more on the lines of baskets and *lambas*,' she said with dignity.

So, while I continued to watch the market, the two of them went off Christmas shopping in that most unlikely of places.

Eventually, they returned laden down with a selection of colourful *lambas* and baskets of all descriptions: some round and fat
with lids, others square, others like gaudy Martello towers –
around the lake the weaving is some of the best in Madagascar
– fine and tight and shiny, like beautiful biscuits with intricately
worked out patterns in different colours. As we examined these
beautiful prizes, Lee returned with her own supply of baskets,
not as upmarket as Araminta's but still very lovely.

At long last, Romulus and Mihanta arrived, full of apologies,
and we set off to the eastern part of the lake. Driving here was
much less depressing than in the western part. In places, the
farms were quite well wooded, whereas on the western side any
tree we saw would be greeted like a long-lost friend. We struck
lucky at the first village we came to. As soon as we stopped in
the main square, Mihanta disappeared like a will-o'-the-wisp
only to reappear ten minutes later carrying a basket containing
a baby Gentle lemur. It would just about have fitted into a teacup
and was a most appealing little thing, with its huge head and
large hands and feet. We had wanted to collect only sub-adult
and adult specimens, but in no way could we bring ourselves to
leave this pitiful scrap in the hands of its present owners. In the
basket with him was only an unhygienic bit of over-ripe banana
and I felt sure – in spite of his owner's protestations to the
contrary – that he was not yet weaned: at that age, a diet of
semi-rotten fruit would be sure to kill him. We purchased him
for a very small sum of money and lectured his erstwhile owners
on the law. Did they not know that it was illegal to kill or capture
these animals? Oh yes, they admitted, they knew that but, as
no one ever came to enforce the law, what was the point of
obeying it? This sort of attitude, which one meets all over the
world, is what makes conservation work so very frustrating.

We were just making our way out of the village when we
were flagged down and another three baby lemurs were produced. They were slightly older than the one we had purchased
and I judged them to be at least partially weaned. Again, we
could not bear to leave them in conditions that would surely
bring about their death, so we bought them and, after another

lecture on the law, we left with four baby lemurs in our possession.

In every village from which we obtained animals we only paid 'recompense' prices, prices so low that the trade in these creatures would not be encouraged, and in every village we carefully and patiently explained the law and showed people documents to prove that we were working with the permission of the Malagasy government to collect the lemurs and set up breeding colonies. How much of what we said sank in, I do not know, but we were meticulous about it.

We drove on to another village where there was a small dispensary at which I hoped we could procure a hypodermic syringe for feeding milk to the unweaned baby. All four of the babies were terrified of the noise that Romulus's car made (as, indeed, we all were), so when we got to Andreba we purchased some milk and a syringe and stopped for an hour during which we fed the babies. They all drank the milk greedily and then the older ones ate some bananas, which was encouraging. Mihanta disappeared once again while the feeding took place, and reappeared with an adult female lemur with a leash around her waist. She had been in captivity for some time and was comparatively tame. Her coat was dull, her teeth were worn and she had a generally apathetic air about her but, nevertheless, we bought her. (Later, it turned out that it was a very good thing we did.) By this time, the four babies had fed well and were sufficiently rested to face the horror of Romulus's engine for the second time. I suggested we make all speed to our hotely, not only for the babies' sake but for my own, as none of the antibiotics I had taken appeared to have had any effect.

We were now in a predicament. We had one adult, one sub-adult and four baby lemurs in our possession and it was not possible to conceal this fact from the management of the hotel. Coward that I am, I dispatched Lee to break the news of this infestation of lemurs to M. le Patron and his wife. To our astonishment, they greeted the news with joy, saying that they were ardent animal lovers, and immediately rented us a room next door to ours, where we could keep our precious charges. It was a small room with a basin, a table and a gigantic double bed. We stripped the bed down to the mattress and carefully covered it with a plastic sheet. The table became the food preparation area and the basin was used for washing dishes. The animals were placed on the bed and various fruit and vegetables piled in baskets under the table. I have not had as much fun disrupting a hotel since, when making a film in Corfu and at the suggestion of the manager (a keen herpetologist), I kept a flock of terrapins in our bath. The shriek of a Greek maid when faced with a bathful of terrapins is as pervasive as the sound of the late Maria Callas treading on a scorpion (though slightly less dulcet).

The following morning, I began to feel that, if anyone sidled up to me and made me an offer of five farthings for all my internal organs, I would accept it without hesitation. As a result, I told Lee that I could not accompany her on a lemur hunt around the lake but would stay at the hotely, lashed, as it were, to the lavatory, and look after our new acquisitions. Aside from my own problems, I felt that our baby lemurs – particularly the smallest – needed feeding at regular intervals. Having fed them all, I took my diary down to the bar and sat there finishing off my notes, being waited on by an enchanting little maid who spoke nothing but Malagasy. In the corner of the bar was a large, loud colour television and, in between serving me drinks, the maid stared at the screen, watching an explicit French soap opera, most of which seemed to take place in bed and involved much moaning and gasping.

Just before lunch, I went up to feed the babies again. The older ones were now lapping up milk greedily from a saucer, but the smallest still needed to be fed with the syringe. He drank until his little tummy was bulging, however, holding on to my hand with a vice-like grip and staring up into my face with wide, golden eyes. At that age, lemurs' heads, hands and feet are wildly out of proportion to their slender bodies and when they move on a flat surface they have the most comical Chaplinesque walk. When they climb into the branches, however, you realize that their outsize hands and feet are the most efficient grasping organs. I had moved the cages on to the double bed so that our youngest acquisition could see the new elderly female (whom we had named Araminta) and I was pleased to hear them exchanging gossip and popping noises.

I returned to the bar, where the soap opera's sexual activities continued enthusiastically, and ordered a bowl of soup with plenty of rice, hoping that this would have a soothing effect on my stomach, as well as some mangoes to dissect for the lemurs. The bar and restaurant had filled up by now and the cacophony of voices added to the grunting and moaning from the television and caused such a din that I decided to repair to our bedroom. Finding I was unable to handle the mangoes and my diary, I indicated in sign language to the little maid that I would like her assistance. With tongue protruding and with the solemn air of one who is carrying a sacred chalice, she picked up the diary and carried it carefully upstairs and into the bedroom. Juggling the mangoes, I followed her. She placed the book reverently on the bedside table, ducked her head, gave me a glittering smile in response to my Malagasy 'misaotra' or thank you, and disappeared. It was some moments later before I discovered that, on leaving, she had turned the key in the door and securely locked me in.

To say that I was in a quandary would be an understatement. The doors and furniture in Madagascar all seem to be made out of a form of wood that in weight and consistency resembles granite, so it was impossible for me to do a James Bond and break the door down by charging it – I would only have dislocated my shoulder. It was useless shouting since the decibel levels of the diners below and the noisy sexual activities in the soap opera would have drowned my cries for succour. I gazed round the room for some weapon with which I could assault the door and found nothing. I went to the heavily barred window, hoping to attract some passer-by's attention. I shouted. Several people looked up and waved to me in a friendly fashion as they walked past. Most of them held up their palms hoping for alms. I sat on the bed and thought about my problem. The baby lemurs needed their food and, almost as important, the lavatory was situated down the corridor.

Suddenly, I remembered having been told that you could open any door, even a Yale lock, with a credit card. My spirits soared.

Out of my wallet I produced my American Express card and attacked the lock. I don't know why I carry this card, since it has been refused by shops and hotels around the world. This occasion was no different. The door refused my card as well. In fairness to American Express, I must admit that Malagasy locks are peculiar. Of massive and ornate design, they were apparently a gift from Mao Tse-tung and have many Chinese peculiarities, not least of which is that you are supposed to put the key in upside down and then turn it from left to right to lock the door and from right to left to unlock. It takes several weeks of experimentation to learn how to get in and out of your hotel room in Madagascar. For the next hour, I paced up and down the room trying to think of a way out of my predicament. All the time, my stomach was informing me in no uncertain fashion that if I did not find my way out fairly soon, it would not be responsible for the consequences. I could have unscrewed the whole lock, but I had nothing to act as a screwdriver.

I was examining the lock and reconciling myself to captivity until Lee returned in the evening, when suddenly the door flew open and there stood the little Malagasy maid. She gave me a wide, warm smile and then, without a word of explanation or apology, she vanished. Hastily, I removed the key from the door to prevent a repetition of my imprisonment and made rapid tracks for the comfort station. My parole had not come a moment too soon.

When I went to feed the babies I found the older ones in a boisterous mood, leaping about in the branches and occasionally thumping down on to the floor and trampling over the youngest, who was looking very dejected. The older babies were in no way bullying him but rather treating him as an inanimate object like a log or a banana, and this was obviously not to his liking. He gazed at me dolefully. I could have put him in one of the lovely little raffia baskets which Lee had obtained, but I felt that he would be even more miserable on his own. Then I had an idea. Gentle lemurs are very social creatures and, as their name implies, are not given to rowdy bickering among their own kind. We had an elderly female (who I suspected was past childbearing) so why not make her a surrogate mother for the baby? The more I thought about it the more the scheme seemed to have merit. I did not know if the ancient female would share my views, but she was comparatively tame and this made matters easier. I lifted the door of her cage and inserted the baby, readying myself for an immediate rescue operation should she show signs of displeasure. The baby took one look at her, rushed across the cage and flung himself on to her – in his enthusiasm climbing right over her head and face before finding the correct niche for a baby lemur, spreadeagled firmly across her chest. She was momentarily startled by this sudden invasion but, to my relief, clasped him in her arms as he burrowed into her thick, warm fur. Of course, she had no milk and the next problem was whether he would leave her in order to be fed. As it transpired, I need not have worried. He tried once to feed from her milkless teats and was given a sharp nip for his pains. After that, as soon as he saw the door of the cage open and Lee's hand with the syringe full of milk, he would scramble off his surrogate mother, stagger across the cage like a dying man in a desert who sees an oasis, fling himself on to Lee's hand and then drink his fill. It was the perfect arrangement: we fed him, she provided him with love and warmth.

Later that evening, the intrepid hunters arrived back tired and thirsty but carrying in triumph two semi-adult lemurs, a male and a female, both in lovely condition. Having fed them and bedded them down, we celebrated. Araminta and I had anti-biotics and whisky and the others had whisky.

I was uncomfortable during the night, with a temperature of 103 and sweating as though newly emerged from a Turkish bath, but in the morning I felt a little better and we decided to have a quick run out to some villages we had not yet visited. At one of these, Mihanta insisted we drive a mile or two up a dilapidated track. Presently, we came to a large mound with a theodolite perched on top. From there we could see parts of the lake proper, surrounded by reed beds and rice paddies. The lake itself did not seem terribly big but it was obvious that before it was clogged by the debris of erosion from the surrounding hills it must have been enormous. Mihanta explained that after heavy rains the water level in the lake rose, flooding the reed beds. When these were cut they formed rice paddies. As the water level of the lake receded it left behind pools which were natural fish traps, giving a rice harvest from the paddies where the reed beds used to be, and a larder of fish in the pools that were left. Owing to the red silt, however, the rich production of Alaotra has dropped and the rice bowl has become depleted. When you compare the figures for the population increase and those showing the drop in rice production over the last few years, the seriousness of the situation is obvious.

Another interesting but depressing change in the life of the lake is the disappearance of the endemic fish. Man, who is forever tinkering with nature because he thinks he knows best, introduced various outside species like tilapia and carp, fish whose ways were so inimical that the local species died out. Nobody knows how many Malagasy species vanished, for no proper study of the lake fauna had been done, but vanish they did, some of them without even having the doubtful privilege of having had a scientific name bestowed upon them.

In a village nearby, Mihanta did his Cheshire cat vanishing act, leaving us (like Alice) with only the memory of his wide beguiling grin, but he soon returned looking very pleased with himself and carrying three raffia baskets with a half-grown lemur in each one. We found ourselves in something of a pickle as now we had exceeded our quota and had ten specimens instead of six. It was impossible to leave any of the lemurs when we knew that they would be on the menu that night in one or other of the village huts.

We wended our way back to the hotely and held a council of war. We had succeeded in what we had set out to do magnificently, for I had thought we would be lucky to obtain a pair of lemurs, let alone ten of these beautiful creatures. The plan had been, of course, to take our furry cargo back to Antananarivo by train. However, Araminta and I were now feeling so rotten that we decided that the best thing to do – rather than face a bone-shaking, twelve-hour train ride – was to send the healthy male members of the party, Edward and Mihanta, off with the adult lemurs on the train while the rest of us flew back with the babies.

Lee carried the babies in individual baskets wrapped in *lambas* and Araminta was festooned with her Christmas presents so she looked like a walking section of the market. Fortunately, for the most part, the Malagasy are a placid people and, moreover, travel with the strangest burdens themselves, so they viewed our eccentric luggage with equanimity. Once we were settled in the tiny plane and had taken to the air, I consulted an English-Malagasy dictionary I had purchased in the hope of taking my mind off my stomach cramps and improving my knowledge of Malagasy which, up until now, extended only to 'good morning' and 'thank you', not enough, I felt, to enable me to conduct an intellectual conversation. Almost as soon as I settled down to learn, I soon found, to my dismay, that this was easier said than done.

Malagasy is a fine, rackity-clackity, ringing language which sounds not unlike someone carelessly emptying a barrel of glass marbles down a stone staircase. It may be apocryphal, but it is said that written Malagasy was first worked out and put down on paper by early Welsh missionaries. They must have greeted the task with all the relish of people who christened towns and villages in their own country with names that seem to contain every letter in the alphabet. The map of Wales is bestrewn with such tongue-twisting names as Llanaelhaiarn, Llanfairfechan, Llanerchymedd, Penrhyndeudraech, and, of course, Llan-fairpwllgwyngyllgogerychwyrindrobllantyssiliogogogoch. So the missionaries, licking their lips, must have approached with zeal the job of making a whole language one gigantic tintinnabula-tion, and they surpassed themselves in the length and com-plexity of their translation. So, when my dictionary fell open at the word 'bust' and informed me that in Malagasy it was '*ny tra tra seriolona voasokitra hatramin ny tratra no ho miakatra*', I was not surprised. It did not, of course, tell me whether it translated 'bust' in the sense of broken, going bust in a financial sense, or a woman's bosom. If it was a lady's bust, however, I decided it would take considerable time to get around to describing and praising other delectable bits of her anatomy, by which time she may well have come to the conclusion that you had a mammary fixation and lost interest in you. A language as elongated as this tends to slow down communication, particularly of a romantic nature.

We arrived safely in Tana and smuggled the babies into the hotel. This time we had commandeered a suite of two large bedrooms and a bathroom. The extra bedroom was needed for storage of all our pieces of animal kit (folding cages and so on) and, in any case, would be useful when the Jersey Channel Television team arrived. Channel Television had, for many years, filmed our exploits in the zoo in Jersey. Now they had a chance to film a real expedition catching Aye-aye and they jumped at it and would soon appear with their complex outfit of everything from film to generators. The adult lemurs from the lake had arrived safely under the tender care of Edward and Mihanta and soon we had them bedded down comfortably at Tsimbazaza Zoo. We decided to keep the babies at the hotel for the time being since they needed feeding so frequently.

The morning after our arrival, I was lying in bed thinking drowsily about getting up and feeding the baby lemurs when I heard a chorus of excited popping noises coming from the room next door, where we had installed our infants in their neat round baskets. The popping noises increased and reached a crescendo. Then came silence. I wondered what on earth our tiny charges were up to. Suddenly, it occurred to me that a cat or a rat may have got into the room somehow and could, at this very moment, be devouring our precious babies. This awful thought galvanized me into action and I leapt out of bed just in time to see Edward (the smallest of the quartet) saunter into the room with his Chaplin walk, all big eyes and innocence. He must have somehow shifted the lid of his basket and escaped. Obviously, he could hear us in the next room and, as we represented provender and he was more than ready for his breakfast, he made his way to us. As I leant over to pick him up, he uttered a bark of horror and fled behind the door. I suppose, from his point of view, it was as terrifying as suddenly being attacked by the Eiffel Tower or Mount Everest. I closed the door to get at him and he

33

immediately went on the defensive, standing on his hind legs, arms outstretched, back against the wall, yapping defiance at me. I scooped him up and when I got him level with my face he started playing with my beard and purring like a kitten.

I put him on my bed with a piece of banana and, carrying this moist trophy he immediately walked over Lee's face in order to eat it in comfort on the pillow. I opened the door and peered into the next room to ascertain how Edward's compatriots were faring and was faced with what appeared to be a sea of baby lemurs. They must have watched Edward's escaping technique with close attention and copied him. It took me some time to round them up and assemble them in a neat circle round a saucer of milk on the bed. I was grateful, though, that they had not decided to explore our equipment because, if they had got in amongst the rucksacks and other gear, the job of finding them would have been as difficult as extricating them from the Hampton Court maze.

'They're adorable little things,' said Lee, as she wiped some semi-masticated banana from the pillow and I mopped up a pool of milk on the bedspread (the babies' table manners left a lot to be desired), 'but I shall be glad when we can pass them over to the zoo for safe keeping.'

'So shall I,' I said, rescuing Edward, who was determined to be the first mountaineering lemur to scale the curtains. 'That popping chorus they indulge in sounds like a perpetual cocktail party.'

Later in the morning, the zoo phoned us to say that they were ready to house the babies and that, to our delight, Joseph Randrianaivoravelona was to look after them. He was one of the first Malagasy students to come and train with us in Jersey and so we knew our boisterous cohort would be in good hands.

Many years ago, it had become abundantly clear to me that the captive breeding of endangered species could best be done in their country of origin. The snag was that in most of these countries no one had been trained in this delicate art and so no one could undertake it. This led us to found our International Training Centre in Jersey in a property adjacent to our zoo. Here, students are taught the day-to-day process of animal husbandry as well as the basic principles of conservation and ecology. Some students are paid for by their governments and others are given scholarships by us. After training with us, they take their expertise back to their own countries and, with our help, set up breeding colonies of their endangered fauna. The scheme has been an enormous success and, as I write, 282 students from sixty-five countries have benefited from the training. One of the spin-off benefits is that the course brings together so many different nationalities and makes the students aware that their particular country is not alone in having the worry of, say, inadequate funds, an implacable bureaucracy, an unsympathetic government, or a population which thinks that the only good animal is a dead one, the only good tree is a felled one. This gives them an important sense of camaraderie and this daisy chain of students around the world no longer feel so isolated. To encourage them to keep in touch, we publish a newsletter especially for our students, called *Solitaire* (another extinct bird like the Dodo), so that they may hear of the problems and progress of other students. It seemed singularly appropriate that Joseph, one of our first Malagasy trainees, should look after our rare collection.

Our training scheme was the first step in the right direction but much more needed to be done. Where were we to set up our breeding colonies in the countries of origin? At first, the obvious answer seemed to be the local zoos. Most zoos around the world were in a pretty dilapidated and seedy condition, through poor funding and sometimes lack of expertise. If these institutions could be brought up to a high standard, then there was no reason why they should not become vital and important links in a chain of captive breeding efforts around the world. Where, however, was the vital money for renovations to come from?

It seemed to me, pondering the problem on a earlier trip to Madagascar, that a great many rich, well-organized zoos in the world were interested in the unique Malagasy fauna and would be willing to assist in its conservation, and that these wealthy institutions could well afford to pay to help their less fortunate colleagues. Together with Lee and my faithful and far-sighted team in Jersey, I worked out a formula which seemed to fit the bill. Firstly, we should set up a group, and each zoo that wanted to join should pay a set annual fee. The accumulated funds should be spent on putting the local zoo back on its feet, helping with expert advice, training staff and rebuilding or renovating cages.

Secondly, after a few years, when the zoo concerned was on its feet and functioning well, the members of the group and the zoo itself would set up joint breeding programmes for the endangered animals of Madagascar. There was one important condition. The animals and their progeny bred at zoos outside the country should remain the property of the Malagasy Government and could be recalled by them at any time. In the Accord that we signed with the Malagasy authorities, we invented this stipulation as a safeguard because many countries felt that outsiders were only interested in grabbing the fauna and running, as it were, and did not have the best interests of the country at heart. Our clear statement of intent was meant to give confidence and to show that in no way would we exploit the country's zoological heritage.

Naturally, when we launched the plan, many zoos showed great interest but in others we were faced with the hysteria of zoo directors with a stamp collector's mentality who could not contemplate a policy of acquiring animals they did not own. However, there was a sensible quorum of directors and zoos who were intelligent enough to see the merits of the idea and the Madagascar Fauna Group was born.

We chose the main zoo in Antananarivo, Parc Tsimbazaza, as one of M.F.G.'s first projects, since breeding units could be built up relatively easily in the capital city. This would not only benefit the animals already living at Tsimbazaza but would be of enormous educational importance. When Madagascar was a French colony, the school system was based on education in France, so Malagasy children were being taught about Renard the fox, rabbits, hares and other creatures not found in Malagasy forests, whereas tenrecs, lemurs, chameleons and tortoises were ignored. When I first went to Madagascar in the 1970s, the only

way an adult or child could learn about local fauna was from a
series of blurred colour drawings on the backs of the boxes of a
certain brand of matches. It was obvious that a living representa-
tive collection of local fauna in the centre of the capital city
could have immense educational potential and the beautiful
park already had a rich and varied collection of indigenous trees
and plants. It was run by an old friend of ours, Voara Randriana-
solo, and his wife Bodo, both of whom loved the park and were
anxious that it should grow into a valuable national collection
of animals and plants.

When the Madagascar Fauna Group was set up we had
already been working with the Randrianasolos for a number of
years to try to help Tsimbazaza find its feet. Two members of
the Tsimbazaza staff (one was Joseph) came over to Jersey for
training and returned carrying with them new experiences of
animal management and knowledge of the hundred and one
things necessary for the setting up of breeding colonies of a wide
variety of creatures. Several members of our own staff were sent
out to work at Tsimbazaza for short periods but, as usual,
finances were tight and progress was slow.

The M.F.G. was lucky enough to engage the services of an
American woman, Fran Woods, who had had a lot of experience
in various zoos. Fran was sent out to advise and work alongside
Voara and his staff for a year during all the different stages of
development and to report back to the M.F.G. on progress and
on the future needs of the zoological park. We had fruitful discussions with Voara and Fran when we arrived in Madagascar
at the beginning of the expedition, and we are confident that,
in a few years' time, Madagascar will have a national zoological
and botanical collection equal to that of any major institution in
the world.

What, meanwhile, would be the fate of our poor persecuted
Gentle lemurs from the vanishing lake? It was quite obvious
from our experiences up there that a great many people had no
idea that this creature was protected, while others knew but
ignored it, for the infrastructure was so poor that it was almost
impossible to implement the law. What was needed was some

sort of campaign, but of what sort and how should we implement it? At that moment, with a vast grin of excitement, Mihanta had his brilliant idea. The children were the key to this, he said, for the parents would listen to the children when they would not necessarily listen to the law. Mihanta's idea was to take, periodically, certain advanced and intelligent pupils from various schools around the lake and transport them by train to the capital city where they could attend conservation lectures and visit Parc Tsimbazaza to see the animals and plants and the museum. Hand in hand with this, we in Jersey would produce a colourful conservation poster explaining the need for protecting the harmless lemur which was found *nowhere else in the world* (a fact which had impressed the people we had talked to). This poster would be hung in all the schools and public buildings and some would be given to the children to take home. The government is desperately trying to get to grips with the problems at Alaotra and to stop the lake from vanishing. Hopefully, if they succeed in their efforts and we succeed with ours, there is a chance that both lake and lemurs can be saved.

We now have, safe in Jersey, the only group of Gentle lemurs in captivity. We trust they will breed and when they do we will distribute their progeny (with the permission of the Malagasy government) to other zoos so that we will not have all our lemurs in one basket. We hope they will go on and prosper both as an educational example of what conservation can achieve and as an insurance of their future existence.

3

An Interlude with Yniphora

Five species of tortoise inhabit Madagascar but the largest and most spectacular is the Angonoka or Ploughshare tortoise (*Geochelone yniphora*). This ponderous animal, sometimes nearly half a metre long and weighing up to twenty-five kilograms (sixty pounds), is only found in the Baly Bay region of the north-west. It has the dubious distinction of being the rarest tortoise in the world. At one time, this creature had a wider range and larger population than it has today and there are a variety of reasons for this shrinking of its range and numbers. The most deadly is the annual burning of the scrubland in which the tortoise lives, which eradicates and alters its habitat. Moving at a plodding speed, these great beasts cannot escape the fires and are roasted alive.

The second threat is thought to come from the introduced African bushpig. These voracious and omnivorous creatures grunt and till their way through the scrubland and, with the delicate sense of smell displayed by their European domestic relations who hunt the delectable truffle, the bushpigs are believed to hunt for the equally delectable (to them) nests of the Ploughshare where they disembowel them and devour the eggs and soft-shelled young with the enthusiasm of a human gourmet faced with a platterful of succulent oysters.

The third threat comes from human beings. Fortunately, the tortoise is not eaten by the tribes in the area. Curiously enough, though, it is kept as a pet and incarcerated in the owner's chicken run in the belief that the presence of the reptile or its droppings in some way prevents the appearance of a cholera-like poultry infection. Whether there is any proof of this we have yet to discover. So the Ploughshare has to contend with the possibility of becoming a pot roast in the fires, having its progeny eaten by pigs, or be taken into a chicken run as a prophylactic for a lot of emaciated fowls.

Now that there are only two to four hundred Ploughshares left these represent problems enough for the species' survival, but it faces one final hazard: if its numbers drop too low the possibility that the males cannot find the females to mate increases. As the whole mating desire appears to be triggered off by the combats between male rivals, it is possible that, as they become more and more scarce, they may have difficulty not only in finding a female but in finding a sufficient number of male rivals to trigger off the mating response.

In 1985, the Trust was asked by the Tortoise Specialist Group of the Species Survival Commission of I.U.C.N. (the International Union for the Conservation of Nature) if we would undertake a rescue operation for the Ploughshare tortoise. We agreed and the project was handed over to Lee because of her deep interest in and knowledge of Madagascar. The first thing she did was employ the services of David Curl, who had done a study on the tortoise in Madagascar and had written an interesting paper on its present status. In it he had mentioned that the *Eaux et Forêts* department of the Government had seven Ploughshares in captivity at a forestry station on the east coast. This was an unsuitable place for them to be kept since, apart from anything else, the climate was wrong and so their chances of breeding were remote. In talks with the authorities, it was agreed that the animals should be moved to a more suitable area and a captive breeding colony set up. We hired David to try to find a site to which we could transfer the tortoises.

After some thought, David recommended the Ampijoroa Forest Station near the town of Mahajanga, which was climatically right and, as a bonus, had some small buildings which could be used by our project. Most helpfully, Air Madagascar gave us free 'tickets' for our precious cargo and the seven tortoises were flown from the east coast to begin their new life much closer to their natural home.

At this point, David had to leave the project to continue his studies and, since there was no one yet in Madagascar who had a first-class knowledge of herpetological breeding, Lee's next job was to find someone in Britain with the expertise who was willing to go and bury himself or herself in the wilds of Madagascar on a minute salary and for an undetermined length of time (tortoises will not be hurried, least of all where their sex lives are concerned). Just as Lee was despairing of finding such a herpetological paragon, Don Reid swam into our lives, a man bearing a remarkable resemblance to the film star Melvyn Douglas and whose great interest in life was all animals and especially anything in the herpetological line, from tortoises to tree frogs. This meant that, once Don was installed, the project could go ahead.

This was Lee's first project and she soon learned that planning a project is one thing, raising funds to start it and to keep it going is quite another. Her phone vibrated like a tropical chorus of frogs and crickets day and night and the bulk of our mail every day consisted of letters to do with the project. I thought of the Ploughshares, clumping slowly through their ever-decreasing habitat, blissfully unaware of the frantic efforts that were being made to try to save them. It is just as well that the poor creatures did not know of all the harassment and difficulties – it might have given them a collective nervous breakdown and they might well have become extinct in consequence.

Finally, the funds were raised and Don sallied forth to Madagascar. The tortoises settled down extremely well, so well in fact that they began breeding during their first year at Ampijoroa. If the breeding continued to be so successful, the next stage would be to plan a reserve for *yniphora* somewhere in its natural habitat. This would mean another tortoise project – more fundraising, more complications as we argued with all and sundry over where the best place would be to have the reserve and worked out the many ways to protect it from pigs, dogs, cattle and humans. But this lay in the future. For the time being, we were content with our early progress.

41

Naturally, since we were in Madagascar pursuing the Aye-aye, Lee was anxious to see for herself how her tortoise project was progressing. So having seen that our Gentle lemurs were safe in the care of Joseph, we flew to Mahajanga where Don met us and transported us the seventy miles to Ampijoroa, which is also the headquarters of the Ankarafantsika Reserve, one of the biggest in Madagascar. Here we met Don's Malagasy assistant, Germain. He was a tiny, slender Malagasy who laughed and grinned at everything that Don said to him, unless it was something to do with tortoises, when his face would become grave and he would listen with great attentiveness. Especially quick to learn, he had already mastered the day-to-day routine of the reptiles' welfare and passed our training course in Jersey with flying colours. As yet, he could not take blood samples or perform some of the other tricky scientific manipulations that are needed for the correct maintenance of the *yniphora*, but you could tell by his quick intelligence that it was only a matter of time before he would be able to handle the whole operation.

Under the shady trees at the edge of the reserve, Don had laid out and built what amounted to a Ploughshare housing development. The pens were simple in construction – thick logs like telegraph poles laid horizontally made up the fence, which did not need to be very high as, obviously, tortoises cannot climb. Each pen had an area with a palm-leaf roof to supply shade should the reptiles wish for it. Alongside the pens was another, much larger, palm-leaf shelter where the tortoises' food was prepared in large stainless-steel dishes full of grasses and vegetables, sometimes covered with raw egg for protein.

Each pen was spacious and could be made three or five times the size to help with the mating procedure by the simple expedient of moving a few logs. The strange protuberance of the shell under the animal's head (which bestows on it the name Plough-share) called an *ampondo* is the animal's fighting gear. It is essential, apparently, for the males to fight in order to be roused to such a pitch that they are overcome with emotion and can mate with the females. A lone male kept with any number of luscious, buxom and voluptuous females (by tortoise standards) just tends to wander round forlornly, ignoring the wiles and manifold attractions of the females, simply because he has no one to fight. To be the only male surrounded by attractive and willing females is a situation, you would have thought, that would bring out the Don Juan in any tortoise worth his salt, but the Ploughshare needs fisticuffs as an aphrodisiac. When the situation is right, however, battle commences and it is a fascinating contest to watch.

The two males, rotund as Tweedledum and Tweedledee dressed for battle, approach each other at what, for a tortoise, is a smart trot. The shells clash together and then the Ploughshares' *ampondo* comes into use. Each male struggles to get this projection beneath his opponent and overturn him to win a victory in this bloodless duel. They stagger to and fro like scaly Sumo wrestlers, the dust kicked up into little clouds around them, while the subject of their adoration gazes at their passionate endeavours, showing about as much excitement and enthusiasm as a plum pudding. Finally, one or other of the suitors gets his weapon in the right position and skidding along and heaving madly he at last overturns his opponent. Then, he turns and lumbers over to gain his just reward from the female, while the vanquished tortoise, with much leg-waving and effort, rights himself and wanders dispiritedly away. Like so many battles in nature, it is merely a stimulus, a trial of strength in which no one is hurt and no gore is shed.

It was not mating time on this visit but we had seen it in previous years. This year, however, we were to see something different and very special – the results of these reptilian jousts.

Don took us over to a special small pen, carefully constructed against hawks, snakes and a local dog, to say nothing of the rapacious *Fosa*, a carnivore like a giant, elongated cat, endemic to Madagascar.

'Well, this is the latest batch,' said Don, with ill-concealed triumph in his voice. He bent over and the next moment he placed in Lee's eager, outstretched hands a quartet of newly-hatched Ploughshares.

'Oh!' said Lee. 'Aren't they adorable?'

Indeed they were. Holding them was like holding four, tiny,

sun-warmed cobbles, beautifully fretted and sculpted by wind and waves. Lee crooned over them, admiring the brightness of their tiny eyes embedded like chips of onyx in their intelligent faces, their sharp, manicured claws like minute golden half-moons, and their sturdy little legs encased in meticulously carved scales like fossilized leaves from a pigmy tree. No matter how comprehensive the reports of the man on the ground are, there is nothing like seeing and holding the fruit of your labours. Taking these almost circular, still-soft fragments of wriggling life in our hands made all the struggles and begging for money, all the persuasion of bureaucracy, all the months of toil and planning fade away. Cupped in our hands, these funny little pie-crust babies represented the future of their race. Guarded from harm, we knew that, ultimately, they would grow into those ponderous adults that, heavy and clumsy as knights in armour, would joust each season for their ladies, so that these extraordinary antediluvian creatures could breed and go lumbering on into new centuries to remind us how the world began and to delight us with their unique shape and habits. Certainly, Lee, Don and Germain had an achievement of which to be proud.

'Come on,' I said to Lee, 'you've crooned over those babies long enough. You'll spoil them if you go on dripping tears all over them.' Reluctantly, she returned the babies to their fortress and we went and sat in the cool, dark shade of the teak trees to drink the babies' health in lukewarm whisky out of cracked glasses and chipped mugs.

Behind the cluster of forestry huts Don had made an attempt at a garden where he was trying to grow various foodstuffs for his charges. It was surrounded by a makeshift fence of branches in an attempt to deter the gourmet enthusiasm of any passing zebu. As I poured out a refill for everyone and gave the toast, 'Tortoises of the world unite, you have nothing to lose but your shells', I saw something white move there out of the corner of my eye.

Looking around, I saw to my delight that we were about to be invaded by one of the Malagasy lemurs I love most: the enchanting, beautiful acrobats of the woods, the Cocquerel's *sifaka*. They have a creamy-white, thick pelt marked in chocolate along the shoulders and thighs, and the fur on the tops of their heads is a rich chestnut that makes them look as if they are wearing little skull caps. Their round golden eyes have a wide-eyed stare which makes them appear slightly demented. But it is the supple agility of their movements which is so extraordinary. As we watched the group, which consisted of six adults, some of the females carrying their tiny, goblin-like babies, they assembled in the trees at the end of the fence. Some were quietly grooming, others sitting in the light of the setting sun, heads back, arms outstretched to gain the maximum benefit from the health-giving rays. After a time, one who was bolder than the rest appeared to volunteer as a scout. He made his way down the tree backwards in human fashion and then dropped on to the fence. Here he sat for a moment, wide-eyed, gazing around him for danger. Then, in a series of bouncing hops that any kangaroo would have envied, he progressed along the whole top rail. Each of these bouncing leaps carried him about six feet and he soon reached the other end of the fence and hurled himself into the safety of the trees, a prodigious leap of about twenty feet. The rest of the troupe, having seen that their compatriot had not been torn to shreds by us or any other lurking predator, made their way on to the fence and bounded along it and leapt into the trees. They moved along through the branches until they were directly above us, and here we were treated to the most spectacular ballet. They leapt through the trees covering thirty feet or more and then simply threw themselves at the branch above us without taking any apparent aim or judging distance. Yet they achieved their target with amazing accuracy. They played around in the trees above us for a few minutes, giving acrobatic displays of such brilliance that they would have had any circus proprietor reaching for his cheque book and contract form. Then, suddenly, they all decided that this particular piece of their habitat had lost its charm and with one accord they went trampolining away through the forest like a white tornado.

Heaving a deep sigh of satisfaction, I turned to Don.

'That was one of the best ballet-cum-acrobatic displays I have ever seen,' I said. 'Their abilities would make even the Russians think twice. Thank you for organizing it just at drinks time.'

'Not at all,' said Don, modestly. 'We men of the forest live as one with the animals and they obey our every command.'

'Less of the bull,' I said severely. 'Where's this swim you promised me?'

We made our way through the trees and down to the edge of the nearby lake, a wide, placid expanse of brown water, rimmed with forest like a green, astrakhan collar. Its water was refreshing, even though it was as warm and soft as fresh milk, but of a completely different colour and composition.

'What about crocs?' I asked, as we floated gently in the coffee-coloured waters.

'A few, said Don, 'but you don't often see them.'

'Well, you and Germain swim ahead of us,' I suggested, 'and then if one of you disappears we'll be warned and can swim for shore.'

'Oh, they're quite harmless,' said Don. 'If the truth be known they're probably more frightened of us than we are of them.'

'I wouldn't bet on that,' I replied. 'The Reverend Sibree waxes eloquent on the subject of crocodiles.'

He had indeed waxed eloquent. In Sibree's day – in the late nineteenth century – there were probably more of these reptiles than there are today, since many have now been killed to make shoes, bags and suitcases for the ladies and gentlemen of Europe, and he devotes some space to them.

These reptiles are so numerous in many parts as to be found a great pest; they often carry off sheep and cattle and not infrequently women and children who incautiously go into or even near the water.

Further on in his excellent book he says:

We soon made the acquaintance with crocodiles, for there was one basking in the sunshine on a sandbank just opposite our starting place. We saw a good many of them during the day, although not as many as other travellers have observed, perhaps twenty or thirty, and some of them quite near enough to be seen

very distinctly. Most of them were light grey in colour but others
slatey, and others again spotted with black. They varied in length
from seven or eight to fourteen or fifteen feet. The head is small
and the back and tail serrated like a great pit-saw. They were
generally lying with the jaws wide open and sometimes near
enough to be splashed by the paddles as we passed them.

Our swim, however, was tranquil and unmolested by the giant
reptiles. We lolled about in the water, chatting about this and
that.

'The trouble with Germain is that he thinks Shakespeare is
funny,' said Don, pointing a toe at Germain's grinning head.

'He thinks *who's* funny?' I asked, puzzled.

'Shakespeare. Every time I start reciting my favourite speeches
out of *Henry V* or *The Merchant of Venice*, he laughs so much he
nearly drowns.'

'Can he understand any of it?' I asked, intrigued.

'Not a word,' said Don, gloomily. 'Imagine going through life
without knowing the Bard.'

'Terrible,' I agreed, as Germain gave me a huge smile and sank
beneath the waters in a cloud of bubbles.

Don had laid on a party that night to celebrate our visit. All the
local villages within striking distance were agog with anticipa-
tion and each small community was going to attend en masse.
A reasonably large flat space outside one of the forestry huts
had been lit with candles and the ubiquitous and invaluable
bushlight or so-called hurricane lamp.

Where, I wondered, would people in remote places be without
this simple but invaluable invention? Its yellow glow, like a
small fat crocus, welcomes everyone back to camp at the end of
a hard day. I have watched women doing the most intricate
embroidery and men carving beautiful figurines by it. I have
watched fat toads gather round it in friendly, gulping conclave,
waiting for the moth bounty it so generously provides with its
gentle light. By this same illumination, I have done operations
that would have made Harley Street shudder: taking fat and
suppurating jiggers from village children's feet; trying to pick,

with the deftness of a pickpocket, ingrained earth and gravel from the woolly scalp of my washerwoman after she had fallen thirty feet on to her head on the banks of the river; trying to put tourniquets on a drunken man who had just amputated three of his fingers with his machete while suffering from a surfeit of palm wine. By its friendly illumination, I have crawled sleepily out of bed in the small hours to bottle-feed everything from duikers to bushbabies, from anteaters to armadillos. A statue ought to be created somewhere to the anonymous inventor of this invaluable aid to those who live in places where electricity exists only in the shape of lightning, and where the moon and the bushlight are the sole dependable source of steady light.

Don went off in a borrowed van to fetch people from outlying villages while the accoutrements of the party were laid out, whisky for us, the local rum (that lights up your stomach and twitches your feet dancewards) and the inevitable Coca-Cola for those who like their rum diluted and for the diminutive guests who were not old enough to be able to cope with the electrifying qualities of the rum. Slowly, the local villagers started to arrive. There was the sibilant whisper of bare feet in the warm dust and brown faces started to surround our pool of light, white teeth flashed, there was the sudden glow of a multicoloured *lamba*, a low murmuration like a hive of sleepy bees, a general air of excitement like children waiting for Father Christmas to arrive. Gradually, as Don ferried to and fro, the crowd grew and so did the noise. Glasses clinked, there were giggles and chatter and, occasionally, a few bars strummed on a *valiha*, that instrument without which no Malagasy party can begin. Related in a distant way to a host of stringed instruments – the zither, the balalaika, the ukulele, the banjo, the guitar – the *valiha* consists of a length of giant bamboo some three or four feet long, which acts as the sounding board. The 'strings' are strips of the thick outer skin of the bamboo, cut with great care and then lifted onto a bridge of wood. Both ends of the strings are still attached to the bamboo itself. When the fingers are run over them, they produce a melodious yet curiously mournful trickle of sound that is delightful and is heard everywhere. A *valiha* is a product of the forest that has been turned into a musical instrument of great purity and so, with the aid of a bamboo and a knife, anyone can own a Stradivarius.

Now, the inhabitants of four tiny villages were around us and the party started to warm up. Four *valihas*, a drum and several flutes started to play a repetitive but sweet harmony. The rum we had brought circulated freely and people started to dance. Soon our little dance-floor was crowded and, with the host of colourful *lambas* worn by both men and women, it was like looking at a moving flowerbed through a kaleidoscope.

The party was a great success, everyone joining in the revelry with high spirits, singing and dancing as the music got louder and faster. At two o'clock in the morning, Lee and I opted for bed but the villagers looked as fresh and eager as the moment they arrived. We left them and went to bed and lay listening to the chatter of happy voices, the plaintive music of the orchestra, the clinking of bottles and the shuffle and thump of dancing feet.

Over our breakfast of sweet, black coffee, biscuits and finger-length bananas with a delicate fragrance, we surveyed the wreckage that was Don.

'And what time did you go to bed?' asked Lee.

'I haven't been to bed,' said Don and took a gulp of coffee and shuddered.

'You mean to say you stayed until the bitter end?' I asked in amazement.

'I had to,' said Don, 'otherwise how were half of these people going to get home?'

'Yes, of course, I'd forgotten you were the taxi service,' I said.

'I wouldn't have minded *that*,' said Don, 'but what I didn't realize was that I'd take ten back to their village and five would stay on board because they liked the ride. I was making twice as many journeys as I had to, until I realized what they were up to. I'd have been ferrying them to and fro until dawn if I hadn't discovered what they were doing.'

'Never mind,' I said consolingly, 'come and visit the crocodiles. I'm told a sharp bit of judo with a crocodile is the best cure for a hangover in the world.'

So we went down to the brown lake's smooth waters. The forest was a million shades of green and dew-drenched. In its depths the coucals were singing seductively to the new day, a lovely cry like their name that ended in a bubbling glissade of notes that made the forest ring, a song as pure and throaty and seductive as a cuckoo's call.

Cooled and refreshed by our swim, we made our way back to the project's headquarters and Lee paid final homage to her strange antediluvian hassocks as they lumbered around their pens looking like clockwork toys.

'So we've bred thirty-one so far?' I asked Don, gently squeezing one between finger and thumb, feeling the softness of his shell, like damp blotting paper. He wriggled indignantly at this insulting action and when I put him down he sped off at top speed and hid under a leaf.

'I think we've got the hang of what they need now,' said Don, 'so we should do even better in the future.'

'Then we'll be knee deep in *yniphora*,' said Lee, happily kissing one of the babies on his nose, to his immense astonishment and annoyance.

4

Jumping Rats and Kapidolo

Getting out of the plane at Morandava was like being plunged into a red-hot sponge. After the pleasant Mediterranean climate of Tana, it was a shock to the system. Lungs protested as they tried to draw in the damp, fiery air and immediately our bodies became drenched in sweat. The sun glowered down on us from a sky that had faded to pale blue. There was not a single shade-giving cloud to be seen, nor was there the slightest breeze to cool us. The baked earth was hot enough to fry a pancake on, and each footstep became a laboured, sweat-provoking chore. It was a day for dreaming about fans revolving like windmills above you, of green, cool water in a river, of the gentle squeak and tinkle of ice in a tall, mist-enshrouded glass, a day in fact for dreaming about all the cooling things we most urgently needed and knew we were probably not going to obtain in the foreseeable future.

We were met by John Hartley, his wife Sylvia, who had recently joined our jaunt, and Quentin Bloxam, bathed in sweat but looking – as always – grimly determined.

'What's it like?' I asked, as we packed ourselves into the Toyota. 'Any luck?'

'We've got two rats and some Kapidolo,' said Quentin, triumphantly.

'Excellent,' I said, enthusiastically. 'I can't wait to see them.'

'What's the camp like?' asked Lee.

'Hot,' said John, succinctly. 'Very hot.'

'Very hot with flies,' said Sylvia. With her pert good looks, immaculate hair and big blue eyes, she did not look as if she had

51

come from a fly-ridden camp in the backwoods, but more as if she had just enjoyed a shopping trip in Bond Street.

'It's the fly capital of the world,' said Quentin, with conviction.

'It can't be worse than Australia, surely?' I protested. They say in Australia that if you see someone walking along constantly waving their hands, it's not because they know everyone in town but because they're ploughing their way through flies.

'Wait and see,' said Sylvia, darkly.

'We've decided, before heading back to fly metropolis to treat ourselves to a bit of civilization,' said John. 'You like prawns, don't you?'

'If suddenly confronted with a well-cooked prawn, I should consider it my duty, out of politeness, to eat it,' I said, judiciously.

'Good,' said John. 'Well, we're taking you to a small hotel along here where the dining room's on the beach, so you always get a breeze. They do the most fantastic prawns.'

'Really stupendous,' said Sylvia.

'Like elephants,' said Quentin, reminiscently.

We drove down the pot-holed road and presently came to the hotel, where we made our way through the garden full of huge cloaks of bougainvillaea and copses of hibiscus. The dining room was a large wooden structure, open on three sides and overlooking a wide, sandy beach where small, white-topped waves broke on the shore with a soothing noise. The dining room was shady and the constant cool breeze from the sea soon dried our perspiring bodies. The *maîtresse d'hôtel* was a large, brown Malagasy lady with a broad, handsome face and a searchlight smile. She soon had a battalion of bottles of beer, misty from the fridge, marching across the table and this was followed by platters of gigantic prawns, sunset red, fat and succulent, accompanied by a gargantuan bowl of rice with an entourage of strange and delicious Malagasy side dishes which included, to my joy, a plate of what I called – for want of a more scientific name – underground peanuts. They are round, smooth, brown or fawn seeds, each about the size of a hazelnut kernel. Cooked in a hot chilli sauce of tomatoes and onions, the *vonja bory*, to give them their Malagasy name, are deliciously nutty and firm and taste

something like starchy dumplings. They are a meal in themselves, so by the time we had done justice to the prawns, rice
and the *vonja bory* we were as replete as we could be, cool, well
fed, lulled by the sound of the sea, ready to face the world with
all its challenges and stupidities. On the other hand, as Quentin
pointed out, a long siesta followed by a swim would be just as
welcome but, reluctantly, we decided that duty called and we
must not tarry too long among the delights of Morandava.

The place where they had set up camp was some thirty miles
outside Morandava in the Kirindy forest, which the Swiss have
leased from the government. The experiments they were carrying out were interesting and, if successful, could be of great
importance to all Malagasy forests. The conventional wisdom in
forestry is to practise 'selective logging', which means that only
trees of a certain size are felled and dragged out. But this method,
however carefully done, affects the ecology of the forest. The
tree, as it falls, creates a false clearing by crushing numerous
saplings. Then, it is dragged through the forest, creating still
further havoc. To simplify the removal of the trees the forest is
divided up like a chess-board by wide pathways or rides as they
are called in England. The whole process is of itself disruptive
and detrimental to a delicate ecosystem and when you add to it
the fact that, generally speaking, no small trees are planted to
replace the giants felled, it is hardly 'rational' use of a renewable
resource.

The Swiss are trying to see if it is possible to replace the felled
trees by young growth of the same species and to reduce the
width of the rides by re-designing the zebu carts used to transport the wood. One of the great problems is, of course, that
most of the tropical species are very slow-growing so, if one is
planning for the future, one must think in terms of great
stretches of time. Madagascar hasn't got a lot of time left. About
ninety per cent of her forest cover has already vanished.

Tropical forests are not as strong a rampart as their massive
trees make them appear. The trees live on a thin skin of humus,
most of which is provided by the tree itself, in the shape of dead
leaves and branches. The forest lives on its own waste products.

Remove the trees, and the sun, wind and rain disperse the shallow topsoil as easily as someone blowing dust from a book. The forest is left with compacted earth or only bedrock on which nothing will grow.

The Swiss plan will work out a sensible way of utilizing the forest by intelligent planning of the felling and replanting. If they are successful in their efforts and the scheme is put into operation there is a chance that what is left of the Malagasy forest will survive and, by wise planning, be a vital resource for years to come, instead of being ruthlessly felled for short-term gain.

This western forest where we were based is different, of course, from the thick, lush, moist forest remnants which are found in eastern parts of the island. Here the trees are not very tall and it is more like a deciduous English woodland. The trunks and branches are predominantly charcoal grey or silvery. The rains were late in coming but a few drizzles had produced a delicate greenish haze on the branches and close inspection showed tiny buds, like minute green spear-heads, forcing their way through the bark.

These dry forests of Madagascar are truly the home of the baobab, the dumpty trees. Massive ones lined the road, their pot-bellies protruding. They stuck through the lesser trees, like an army of Chianti bottles, eighty feet or more high, their bulbous bellies the circumference of a small room. Their ridiculous little twisty branches made them look like someone who has washed their hair and can't do a thing with it. What terrible sin had they committed, I wondered, to enrage the Almighty so much that as punishment, he tore them from the newly-created earth and somersaulted them, as legend has it – their roots in the air, their branches underground – so that they were forever destined to be the upside-down tree.

There are lovely trees in Paraguay and Argentina called *palo boracho* – the drunken stick – which are beautiful in their rotundity, but their tummies lack the swelling Falstaffian magnificence, the pure anti-dietary bulge of the baobab. They are, of course, stationary when you see them by daylight but one imagines that at night by the crisp, white light of the moon they uproot themselves ponderously and hie themselves to some secret grove where, under the influence of good, sweet, black rum, they gurgle gossip to each other. One of the saddest sights I have seen was in the south of drought-ridden Madagascar where, in a desperate bid to save their cattle which were dying of thirst, the people had felled giant baobabs and hacked their silvery hide off so that the zebu could get at the fibrous, moisture-filled interior. Each tree had taken maybe a hundred years to grow and was swiftly felled to become a sort of cattle trough. Even in death the baobab's last gesture was a benign one.

As we progressed along the dusty red road, the warm wind of our progress adding to our discomfort rather than alleviating it, suddenly we came upon a small lake among the baobabs, fringed with reeds, grasses and papyrus, its jet, shiny waters emblazoned with water-lily leaves like great seals. I was delighted to see several jaçanas or – to give them their better and more fitting name – lily-trotters inhabiting this small lake. They are aristocratic birds that add elegance and beauty to any stretch of water, large or small, as long as they have something to walk on. With their long, delicate, artistic toes they made their way slowly over the jade-green lily pads, pausing now and then to peck with speed and accuracy at a beetle or a tiny mollusc who had been ill advised to crawl out of the safety of the water. On the banks grazed Egyptian geese, stocky, phlegmatic and looking as though they were dressed in brown tweeds. Over the little lake flew squadrons of bee-eaters, decked out in vivid shades of green, their curved black beaks flashing as they made aerial attacks on the numerous dragonflies that rushed past on rustling, glittering wings. In the clusters of ridiculous branches on top of each baobab, a group of Vasa parrots sat, browny-olive green and unspectacular for parrots, but somehow comforting in their sober but delicate feathering, so unlike the garish glitter – a Woolworth's jewellery-counter effect – of a macaw or of some of the Australian parakeets.

On the far side of the lake, we could see colonies of weaver-birds in the almost bare trees, busy in their villages of round, basket-like nests. It always amazes me that these stumpy little birds can weave the magical nests, which decorate the trees like a crop of strange fruit, with only beak and claws. Further along the road, we disturbed two hoopoes, splendid salmon-pink and black birds with Hiawatha head-dresses and long, curved, scimitar-like beaks. They flew fifty yards down the road and settled again in the red dust, spreading their crests as a conjuror fans a deck of cards.

Soon, we left the road and drove down one of the transects through the forest. This was narrower than the main road, so one could see more closely into the forest on each side. Huge *Oplurus* lizards hurled themselves across the road in front of us, nine inches long, clad in shining caramel and golden-brown coloured scales, tails bristling with sharp spikes, looking like a collection of medieval warriors. One of them was so busy digging a hole in the red earth that it did not rush away as its compatriots had done but continued stolidly with its excavation. We watched it for some time, wondering if it was digging for insects and their larvae or – since it was the breeding season – preparing a hole for its eggs. It had chosen a rather dangerous location for its nursery if it was one since, although the transect could hardly be called a teeming thoroughfare, lorries passed along it carrying tree trunks and so the chances of the nursery caving in and crushing the eggs were not remote. However, after a few more minutes' digging, it suddenly lost interest and, without a glance at the Toyota's wheels just two feet away, it swaggered off into the undergrowth.

We turned off into a sizeable clearing where there was a scattering of reed and bamboo huts for the forestry workers, a large branch-roofed area with hammocks for the workers and a large bamboo hut and a veranda, on which we stored our equipment, cooked, ate and read or wrote. Alongside this John and Quentin had erected their tents and our very posh new one, which consisted of a double bedroom (which could accommodate four if one needed it) and a sort of large porch where we could stack our gear. A bath house and latrine had also been constructed out of bamboo and reeds. Bath house is perhaps a rather grandiose name, conjuring up visions of gleaming taps and baths and heaps of gigantic, white, woolly towels like a convention of polar bears to dry on. The truth was an antediluvian tin bucket and a tin can for throwing water about. As the water had to be ferried from a stream several miles down the road, our use of this precious liquid had to be circumspect but, at least, none of us became odoriferous.

The sun beat down on the forest, burning with the heartlessness of the Inquisition. Any breeze was shredded and strangled amongst the trees and died before ever reaching the clearing. We had settled in and had a lukewarm swill which, if anything, excited our sweat glands to even greater efforts. Now, we went to the communal veranda where the hurricane lamps glowed and the flames of the cooking fire nearby sent shadows flickering to and fro, making the whole scene tremble and dance in the drifts of smoke.

Crouched over the fire and producing the most mouthwatering scents from his labours, was Monsieur Edmond, a Government forestry agent, whose knowledge of the forest and its ways was invaluable to us, as were his abilities as a chef. He was a quiet man who seldom spoke unless spoken to, and seemed – Malagasy fashion – to drift about aimlessly, although he managed to get everything accomplished with the minimum of fuss. He presented us with a delectable chicken stew and followed it with sunset-pink papaya which he had somehow conjured up in the fruitless forest. The full moon, like a huge silver medallion, rode in the velvety black sky and shone so brightly that you could read a book by it: I know, because I did.

Curled up in our tents, covered only by multicoloured *lambas*, we listened to the night orchestra from the forest around us. The Vasa parrots – in a most un-parrot-like way – sometimes spend a part of the hours of darkness singing songs to each other and that first night they were very vocal for an hour or so. Their voices were so penetrating that they drowned the other forest sounds. However, when they stopped we could tune in to the noises of the other inhabitants. There was, as always, the gentle background music of insects, popping, tweeting, buzzing, sawing, trilling, tinkling and burping. But over this sibilant tapestry of sound came clearly the voices of *Microcebus*, the Mouse lemur, smallest of all the lemurs: two would just fill a teacup to over-flowing. They are dainty little things with grey-green fur, huge golden eyes and pinkish hands, feet and ears, all rose-petal soft. They uttered penetrating squeaks and trills and when they encountered another of their kind – presumably trespassing – a great angry flood of Lilliputian invective could be heard as they scolded each other among the moonlit branches.

We could hear the *Lepilemur* which came quite close. Indeed, two of them were singing in the trees that shaded our tent, harsh staccato screams of the most unattractive sort. We were glad when they moved on. For some reason known only to zoologists, these have been christened Sportive lemurs – one can only suppose because of their habit of jumping upright from tree to tree. There are six sub-species, including one with the imposing name of Milne Edwards Sportive lemur, a name which can only have come out of *Debrett's*. Because they feed mostly on leaves, which supply them with only low energy, it is thought that they digest their food by fermentation, then excrete the nutrients and eat their own faeces, thus assimilating 'recycled' nutrients. These rather cat-like creatures are nocturnal and arboreal, with thick brownish fur and large ears and eyes. They spend the daylight hours curled up in a hollow tree. When night falls they take to the trees and are Sportive, making an unholy row with their macabre chants.

The following morning, a crestfallen Q discovered that the two Giant Jumping rats that had been caught had both escaped in the night. It did not seem possible that such bulky animals, with their big heads, could have squeezed through the bars of our collapsible cages, but they had. On a collecting trip such as this one learns constantly that animals – not having read the right books – will astound and amaze by always doing the most unexpected things. I have even had a vanished animal (after a disappearance of a few hours) return to camp and break back *into* the cage from which it had escaped. So we had a gloomy breakfast and, then, before the fly population really woke up, we went to visit the trapline.

The road to where the traps had been set was wide and comparatively smooth and formed a wonderful basking and hunting area for dozens of *Oplurus*. Some were huge, old and stocky with spikes on their tails that made them look as if they were dragging Victorian pincushions after them. It was also a good area for the hoopoes, of which we saw several, beautiful in their salmon, white and black plumage and their fan-like feathered crests making them look as if they were going on the warpath against all insect life. As we walked through the forest we disturbed a small group of trampolining *sifaka*, that bounded off ahead of us but stopped periodically to watch us with an interest not unmixed with alarm just as villagers in a beauty spot view the arrival of a bus-load of tourists.

The homes of the Giant Jumping rats were large and very conspicuous and the hillocks of soil around the mouths of the holes indicated that they must be fairly extensive. John and Q explained that, at first, they set the trap and wedged it over the entrance but they found that the rats simply burrowed round or under the trap with great skill. The new method, which had proved successful, was to sink the trap a trifle and surround it with a fencing of branches hammered into the ground so that the rats were faced with an impenetrable wall of wood and were thus forced to enter the trap if they wanted to leave their nests. Strangely enough, it never seemed to occur to them that they could escape by digging another burrow further back from their front door.

Normally, visiting a trapline is a boring routine and one's hopes are only buoyed up by the thought that surely there will be *something* in the next trap. The sun was now cresting the tree tops and the forest was getting breathlessly hot. There was not the smallest noise and the trees were unruffled by any breeze – it was like walking through an oil painting. Presently, we came to the first trap under a small tree and, to our amazement and delight, sitting in it and looking faintly bewildered, was a Giant Jumping rat. We dislocated the trap from its attendant branches and lifted it out. Our prize, though slightly alarmed, seemed on the whole to take the whole process fairly phlegmatically. With great care, we transported it back to the Toyota and, while the others went off to inspect the rest of the trapline, I remained behind to gloat over our capture.

It was about the size of a small cat, with a very long, thick, bare tail, large but delicate pink feet and huge pinky-grey ears like Arum lilies. Its face, at first glance, looked strangely un-rat-like and rather square, resembling those blunt-faced horses you see in Roman sculpture. It had a mass of stiff, white whiskers, through which it peered like someone looking through a lace curtain. I endeavoured to cement our friendship by giving him a small section of sugar cane and he looked at me with an expression of horror, like a world-famous gourmet who has been served a live, raw lobster by the chef.

Like so much of the Malagasy fauna, these huge rats are unique to the island and, as far as is known, only found in this one small section of forest. They are in a genus all of their own and, having such a limited distribution, its future is, to say the least, bleak, for the felling of the forest continues apace.

As far as I know, the only study that has been undertaken to try to find out about the private life of this strange rodent was a ten-week expedition led by James Cook in 1988. Among other things they discovered that the home of the Vositse, to give it its charming Malagasy name, generally has several entrances, most of which are blocked with debris. When the Vositse is at home but not receiving, the tunnel in use is blocked with freshly dug mud. In many cases, a pair or a threesome of parents and young inhabit these burrows. The animal is strictly nocturnal, sallying forth in the moonlight to forage for fruit, flowers and the tender bark of baby trees. According to Cook, when it leaves its burrow it does so with a mighty bound, propelled by its powerful hind legs. Then, it sits down and has a thorough cleaning session. This is very puzzling behaviour since, if bounding out of its nest is meant to confuse a predator patiently waiting outside, why sit down near the nest and commence an elaborate toilet which requires concentration? However, in my experience, as most of the mammal fauna of Madagascar are more than slightly dim-witted, there is probably no explanation.

The others returned to report that all the other traps were depressingly empty, so we decided to take our one Vositse back to camp where a large travelling cage had been prepared for him, so lashed about with wire that it looked as impregnable as the Bastille. As we were driving back, assuring each other that one Vositse was better than none at all, Q suddenly uttered a yelping, yodelling cry like the mating call of a Brontosaurus and rammed on all the brakes, making us thrash to and fro like a Punch and Judy show caught in a hurricane. I was convinced that he must have been bitten by one of the more malevolent insect inhabitants of the forest, but I was wrong.

'I think,' he said, in agonized tones like one who has just discovered that he has lighted the kitchen fire with an original Shakespeare manuscript. 'I think I have run over a Kapidolo.'

We all recoiled, bristling with horror at this revelation.

'How could you?' said Lee. 'Poor little thing.'

'The idea is to catch them, not kill them,' I pointed out, acidly.

'Well, I couldn't help it,' said Q, aggrievedly, 'they have no business walking about on the road.'

'And it wasn't even using a pedestrian crossing,' said John, *sotto voce*.

'You'd better get out and have a look,' I suggested.

He left the Toyota and made his way back down the road as if he was walking in a State funeral. Then he gave a shout of joy and came hurriedly back to us, carrying an unscathed Kapidolo in his hands. When young, these are probably the most beautiful of tortoises though, unfortunately, as they get older their carapaces compress and become oval and the coloration can become a drab grey. In contrast, the young are a riot of colour, their shells marked with chestnut, black and bright yellow. On the head, between the bright eyes and the upper lip is a creamy yellow marking, which makes the animal look as though it is wearing a long moustache of the sort that used to be favoured by our great-grandparents. This one must have been a couple of years old and was still in his radiant, circular, infant shell.

The Kapidolo, or Flat-tailed tortoise, is a strange and lovely little creature about which little is known. It inhabits only a small area in the dry western forest, which has two seasons: the rainy, warm one with the hottest temperatures creeping up to

45°C, which lasts three to five months; and the cool, dry season lasting seven to eight months. They seem to be most active during and after downpours of rain whereas in the dry periods (and at night) they retreat to the heavy leaf litter on the forest floor. They are thought to lay a single, rather large egg, but no one knows how many clutches they produce in a year. It is thought (though no one is sure) that the Kapidolo aestivates below ground during the prolonged dry period and probably digs itself out in order to breed in the rainy season. As with so many creatures, not only in Madagascar but all over the world, we know very little about their private lives and are killing them off before we can find out. The forest we were in is shrinking because the people cut it for firewood and to open pasture lands. When the forest goes, the people will suffer and the Kapidolo and Vositse will disappear, having no ability to find alternative accommodation.

When we got back to camp, we got our charges safely installed and thought that we deserved a beer. The flies joined us. I had thought that the team's complaints at the quantity of flies were an exaggeration, so I was shocked to find that, if anything, their description had been understated.

Firstly, there were the houseflies. At least, I suppose that's what they were. After pouring out a beer and putting the cap back on the bottle only to find that ten flies had committed mass suicide in my glass, I became too dispirited to try to identify them. They were plump and about half as big again as the housefly that causes such alarm in the kitchens of Europe. They took their job to be with us from sun-up to sundown very seriously. The speed with which they could get themselves into a glass of beer or on to a plate of food had to be seen to be believed. The tent poles were black with them, the table top a black moving tablecloth of them. Many of them, when off duty, came and hummed the latest fly pop song in your ear and neither the tune nor the lyrics were more intelligible or less irritating than the average human pop song. They accompanied this serenade by mountaineering up legs, arms, face or any other exposed bits of the anatomy. They had a particularly joyous time when they found someone defenceless in the bathhouse or the latrine.

As if these ministrations were not enough, when the sun was really high, gaping down on us like a dawn bread oven, the flies were joined by the sweatbees. Tiny, rotund and glossy black with gauzy semi-transparent wings, these insects were, if anything, more irritating than the flies. They appeared by the hundred, as silently as shadows, and descended on us in droves. Their desire was for moisture and, of course, under that blistering sun, we sweated continuously and we and our clothes represented manna from Heaven for these tiny creatures. They would settle on us in clouds until our arms, legs and face were so covered with the multitude that we looked as if we were suffering from a severe case of chickenpox. In their greed for the moisture we were exuding, they would try to crawl into our ears, up our noses or, most irritating of all, endeavour to get into our eyes. Killing them gave little satisfaction. So drugged and drunk with having found such an oasis, they crawled, stupefied, upon us. It was possible to destroy fifty or more at one slap but their place was immediately taken by fifty of their compatriots, and the maddening, tickling sensation recommenced. I have often thought that if you pegged a spy out naked in the sun in a sweatbee-infested area, you would get a confession in a trice without the vulgarity of bloodshed.

Slightly later in the day, when the houseflies and the sweatbees had driven us mad, the horseflies would arrive. They were fast, silent and could land so delicately that we were unaware of their arrival. However, each one appeared to be equipped with chainsaws instead of jaws so we were not left long unappraised of their presence. The sudden agony as they pierced the skin felt as if some malignant millionaire was extinguishing a large and expensive Havana cigar on the exposed parts.

The irritating thing about all these noxious insects is that they are so fascinating. Look at a dismembered housefly or mosquito under a microscope and immediately you become captivated by the architectural beauty of their construction. The compound eye of the housefly, for example, is a miracle of design. The delicacy of the wings of some of these insects under the microscope show stained-glass windows more beautifully wrought than anything to be seen at Chartres Cathedral. Indeed, once you have seen the component parts of some of these creatures magnified and studied their incredible intricacies of design, you have a faint, guilty qualm at swatting one and crushing such a structural miracle. The fly family is, of course, an enormous one spreading all over the world. They can live in all the places where man can, and live and rear their young in habitats in which man could not survive, let alone produce progeny. The Shoreflies live and breed in brine so salty you wonder how the young can cope. Other species, for reasons best known to themselves, inhabit hot springs in Iceland, America, Japan and New Zealand, their young living happily in water temperatures that climb up to 55°C. In California – where else – there is a species of fly that lives in lakes of crude oil, the larvae breathing through a tube, a sort of aqualung. When they feed on dead insects, they take oil into their systems as well as food, but by an extremely clever piece of internal engineering, only the food is digested and not the oil.

The list of what the fly family and their young can feed on is astonishing and seemingly endless, ranging from cow dung, rotting flesh, pus and the sap of diseased trees, to more savoury things like narcissus and onion bulbs, asparagus and carrots. The amount of other creatures they prey on, both for food and as a parasite, is extraordinary. The young of the Cluster fly take up their abode in earthworms, other species live in bumble bees and yet others in various caterpillars. As parasites, they prey on anything from man downwards. Fruit flies can cause the unpleasant disease called yaws and, by feeding on the moisture in the eye, can cause conjunctivitis. The Skipper fly, a gourmet among these insects, likes high-quality cheese, such as Gorgonzola or Stilton in which to rear its young. Some iron-willed gourmets insist that a cheese is not ready for consumption unless it heaves and trembles with baby Skipper fly maggots. Few would be so case-hardened, however, if they knew that the maggots are impervious to human digestive juices and may go on living happily inside the gourmet's tummy until their vigorous activities cause severe inflammation of the stomach's mucous lining.

64

The eating of parasites is not confined to civilized Europe. In North America, a kind of Snipe fly, whose families congregate under bridges to drop the larvae before they die, are collected by certain Indian tribes and baked into the Red Indian equivalent of a hot cross bun. One fairly horrifying parasitic fly in the house-fly group lays eggs on an unfortunate – and presumably absent-minded – toad. When the larvae hatch, they take up residence inside the nasal cavity and there, not content with destroying the mucus membranes, go on to eat away the whole front of the unfortunate amphibian's head. (Another species in North America called the Screw worm attacks human beings in the same way and with the same disastrous and horrifying results, if not treated.)

Flies, believe it or not, have their charming, whimsical and useful side, as well as a macabre one. One of the Pomace flies, for example, enabled a major breakthrough to be made in our knowledge and understanding of genetics, so it was and is of the greatest importance to mankind.

The Termite fly, as well as having an extraordinary life history, repays the creature it exploits. Originally, the flies are males but, later, by some insect alchemy they become female. They lay only one large egg at a time and then another extraordinary piece of witchcraft takes place. The fully-grown larva soon hatches and *within a few minutes* it turns into a pupa, surely one of the most hurried life histories in the animal kingdom. Of course, the fly lives in the termite colony and feeds on the ter-mites' eggs but the termites adopt a live-and-let-live policy for the fly repays them. At the end of its ponderous body are some-times yellow tufts which produce a secretion that the termites consider to be a delicacy and so, working on the old biblical principle that you should not muzzle the ox that treadeth out the corn, the termites tolerate their strange guest and its minor depredations among its eggs.

Some of the Danceflies have a charming ritual for seducing an attractive female. The would-be courtier catches another insect and wraps it in a sort of silken wedding veil it manufac-tures from its body. He takes this gift and dances with it in front of the lady of his choice and she, overcome by the graceful generosity of his attentions, becomes immediately receptive. While she eats this provender the male mates with her. In one species, the males, calculating and hard-hearted brutes, have discovered that their females are much more easily seduced. None of this exhausting running about catching insect presents for the chosen one; he simply takes the veil and dances with that. The female, dazzled by the implications of the veil, works herself up into a state of pre-marital bliss. Then the male throws aside the veil, presents himself in his true colours and the female falls victim to his lust. Life among the flies can be as complex and unreal as any TV soap opera.

During the next few days we added steadily to our collection of Kapidolo. The slight rainfall just before we came had enticed them out of hiding and they were trundling about the forest floor and taking their lives in their hands by slowly crossing the logging roads that crisscrossed the area. We were also lucky with the Jumping rats and had soon caught our quota of three pairs, all of which had settled down splendidly in their new homes and on their new diets. It is curious that the scant literature on this beguiling beast makes no mention of their vocalization, for their growls, hisses, yaps and deep sighs soon became part of the wild chorus around us as soon as the sun had set.

On the last morning, we were a bit late setting out into the forest and when we got to the trapline the sun was up, fierce and implacable, crisping the forest into kindling. I begged off going round the trapline and said that I would wait by the road and occupy myself with some bird-watching.

The voices of the others had scarcely died away when the tangle of creepers that adorned the trees above me was visited by a group of Souimanga sunbirds, a slender scrap of a bird with a curved black bill like a scimitar. Its head, chin and throat were a vivid, glittering, metallic green and on its grey-brown back were patches of metallic purple. The breast was glittering blue, edged with red and bright yellow and the tail was green. It was as bright and gay as any gypsy caravan and it lit up the leafless vine it was investigating. The sunbirds are, of course, the African answer to the hummingbird and some are as beautiful as their

South American counterparts. The ones a few feet above me were hunting insects, for there were no flowers on the vine from which to sip nectar. They flew in rapid darts, too fast for the eye to follow, weaving strange geometrical patterns through the branches. They would suddenly come to a stop on blurred wings and peck at an insect too minute for my eyes to discern without a hand lens. The little flock kept in touch and presumably reported progress by a series of sharp sibilant little cries. Soon they had denuded the vine of its insect inhabitants and they moved off into the forest like a miniature firework display.

My next visitors were eight Vasa parrots, endearing birds with rounded tails and pale horn-coloured bills. They arrived vocally and, for a parrot, quite musically, flapping and gliding their way into a fairly large tree some fifty yards away. There was no fruit in the tree nor any other edible substances so I got the impression that they used it more in the nature of a gymnasium, hopping from branches, hanging upside down and having mock battles. They accompanied all this activity with raucous, cackling cries or melodious pipings. They were loud, happy and amusing birds to watch.

I had just been driven back into the red-hot interior of the Toyota by the attentions of the sweatbees when I had another visitor, a remarkable one that I never thought I would be able to see. A flash of russet red caught my eye in the bushes some six feet in front of the vehicle and, suddenly, from out of the undergrowth, silent as a cloud shadow, came a *Fosa* which walked languidly to the middle of the road and sat down. There was no mistaking that slouching, indolent, cat-like gait. I was observing the largest carnivorous mammal in Madagascar, looking very like a young puma and with a puma's walk. When it got to the middle of the road, it sat down some ten feet away from the Toyota, of which it took no notice at all, and remained immobile for a minute or two. It was relaxed and perfectly at ease: no furtive glances over its shoulder, no ear twitches, no tensing of the muscles. It looked as if it had been invited. Since it seemed to be happy and at home, I relaxed too, moving my cramped legs gently to a more comfortable position.

The *Fosa* had a long, athletic-looking body and an inordinately long tail. Its head seemed small in comparison to the rest of its body and reminded me of the ancient Egyptian carvings of sacred cats. Its fur looked dense and sleek and was a beautiful, warm honey-gingerbread colour. It was, after all, carrying the banner of the lion, the tiger and the jaguar, to name but a few of the host of beautiful carnivores found worldwide and so, to be one of their company, it behove it to put on a bit of side. It sat, silent and unmoving for a few minutes, and then commenced to groom itself thoroughly as a cat does, lifting its plump paws to be licked and have the odd burr nibbled away, stretching its hind legs out to receive a wash, curry-combing its thick tail assiduously. The whole process took perhaps five or six minutes and it was wonderful to watch an animal totally unaware of my presence or, if he was aware of it, giving no sign, ignoring me as an aristocrat would be unaware of the presence of a peasant.

Having repaired the minuscule damage which only he could discern on his immaculate fur, he sat upright again, sighed, yawned prodigiously with a flash of white teeth, tested the wind and, then, slowly and gracefully, he crossed the road and disappeared into the forest, his immense sickle of a tail swinging from side to side like a bellrope behind him. I heaved a sigh of deep contentment. To have spent ten minutes with such a rare and beautiful creature was a privilege. Yet the Malagasy dislike and fear the *Fosa* for, they assert, it is quite fearless and will attack zebu calves and man himself if provoked. It may be true, but my *Fosa* looked benign and noble and as if, were he deferentially approached, he would curl up at your fireside, a large, gentle, honey-coloured adornment to your hearth.

I had thought that I had been given my fill of good luck for our last day but more treats were in store. As we were driving back to camp, we came upon a troupe of eight *sifakas* relaxing in the sun-speckled shade of the trees some twenty feet from the road. They were so perfectly grouped and exhibited so many different forms of behaviour that you suspected that they had just signed a very lucrative contract with the BBC and were in the middle of a rehearsal. One sprawled lengthways along a branch, feet and arms hanging flaccidly. Occasionally, he would open his eyes and survey us without interest. Once, he made lethargic attempts to swat a large, blue butterfly, which was flitting around in that indecisive way that butterflies have, but he failed to connect. Two were locked in mock mortal combat, throwing their arms round each other, biting gently and then leaping away. Above them, four members of the troupe were sun-worshipping, with their heads back, arms widespread, looking ridiculously like a travelling opera company singing one of the more difficult parts of the Ring Cycle. In a patch of shade a female sat, her woolly baby on her lap, carefully examining it to make sure that it was unblemished by ticks or burrs or anything else injurious to its well-being. Like all infants, the baby was more interested in trying to climb on to its mother's head so that it could reach up and join the two adults who were doing battle. We spent some time with this enchanting group, photographing them and watching their antics. They took no more notice of us than if we had been a herd of zebu. At last, reluctantly, we left them and they watched our departure with incurious golden eyes. It was salutary to know that we were much more interested in them than they were in us.

The next day, we left Morandava with its gently roasting forest and its superfluity of flies. We had been highly successful and had caught almost everything we wanted. Now we only had the tricky job of getting all back safely to Jersey. I was sorry that there had been no rainfall before we arrived to green the forest, for I felt it would be a nice, friendly place, full of fascinating animals, if it had only been dressed in a few leaves. True, its nudity allowed one to see more in the bare branches but a wardrobe of leaves might have gone a long way to sheltering us from sun. As we bowled down the red, dusty road between the army of stalwart baobabs, a flock of Vasa parrots flew overhead shouting goodbye from the gentian-blue vault of the sky.

The Hunt Begins

Our search for the beast with the magic finger started with an argument which, unfortunately, I won. We were sitting in the Hotel Colbert's bar, waiting for the Jersey Channel Television team to arrive to film us, poring over maps and discussing the route to our destination, some 350 miles from Antananarivo. Firstly, we would have to go due east towards Tamatave on the coast. We knew that this road was a good one because Tamatave was an important port and the Malagasy needed to keep it in reasonable condition. After this, the trouble would begin when we turned northwards and had to travel a rough road with a whole series of river crossings aided only by unpredictable ferries. As the road ran along the edge of the sea we would have to contend with not only the wayward currents of the rivers but the tides as well. The trip boded to be interesting.

'I do wish you'd be sensible and fly,' said Lee. 'You can be picked up in Mananara and driven out to wherever John and Q have decided to make base camp. To drive up there is going to play havoc with your hips.'

My hips, which had been my stalwart companions for sixty-odd years, had recently played a dirty trick on me and developed arthritis, necessitating their removal, banishment and replacement with steel and plastic. The X-ray photographs of my hips after the operation looked like one of the less salubrious barbed-wire entanglements from the First World War. They behaved in this dastardly way while we were filming our television series in Russia, finally collapsing when we were up in the tundra, only 900 miles from the North Pole. Our director had found a magnificent patch of miniature wild flowers some five hundred yards from our camp and he wanted me to do a 'piece to camera' sitting on this lovely, colourful carpet. As the tundra consists of solid ice with a covering of moss and pigmy bushes, it is about as safe to walk upon as a skating rink. I told our director that I simply could not walk that distance when I was in such pain. He went away, crestfallen, and there was a long consultation with the Russians. Then the helicopter which had transported us to this wild and remote spot was started up, I was tenderly transported to it and was flown the five hundred yards, tenderly extracted from the helicopter and deposited among the flowers to do my piece, then equally tenderly transported back to camp. It is the only time in my life that I have felt like Elizabeth Taylor.

My new hips meant that I could walk without agony but I had to be careful not to subject them to too much strain or they protested with vigour. They were a constant and irritating reminder that one was not growing younger, regardless of how one may feel inside.

'Look,' I said, 'everybody we've talked to said the road was O.K. I mean, most of it runs along the edge of the sea and it's flat for Heaven's sake.'

'Everyone says the road is awful,' said Lee, stubbornly, 'and it will affect your hips, I'm sure.'

John and Q, natural cowards, evinced enormous interest in their empty glasses and hoped they would not be drawn into the altercation.

'What do you think, John?' asked Lee. John took a deep breath and gave one of his masterly fence-sitting replies which would undoubtedly have deposited him in the House of Commons, had he taken up politics.

'Well, some people say the road is good, other people say it's bad. Unless we actually travel it, I don't see how we can know. On the other hand, if Gerry wants to go by air it would be comfortable, but if he wants to risk the road, er . . . er . . . well, I think it's a decision only he can make,' he ended lamely.

Lee gave him the sort of look on which eggs are fried.

'Good, then that's settled. Let's have another round of drinks,' I said, cheerily.

'You'll regret it,' said Lee and, to my annoyance, she was right.

The next day, the television team arrived and, for a brief period, chaos reigned as their strange and highly diverse gear was extracted from the eager fingers of Customs, brought to the hotely and piled high in an adjacent room. Later, when each piece of equipment had been unpacked and closely scrutinized to make sure it had not disintegrated during the flight from Jersey, we all repaired to the bar to fortify the team and lay plans. There were, of course, a hundred and one things to be done: visiting the appropriate ministries; picking up last-minute items from the *zoma*; and having last-minute drinks with friends whose tales of horror on the roads (and particularly our road) grew more fearsome and unbelievable as the alcohol flowed freely.

We knew most of the team of old, for they were always popping up to the zoo to film a recent birth or arrival and had made an excellent educational series on our work. There was Bob Evans, our producer, small, neat, with sparkling brown eyes, as pert as a spring robin. The cameraman, Tim Ringsdore, had tight, curly hair, slender good looks and an elegant and well-cosseted moustache lying on his upper lip like a rare moth. If he had had a straw boater, knife-edged white flannels and a striped blazer, he was the sort of 'nut' who, in Edwardian times, would have propelled his lady in a punt down the Thames and, in a suitably shady and remote spot, serenaded her with his ukulele.

Our sound recordist, Mickey Tostevin, was so beefy that he made Q look like a reject from a home for consumptives. His auburn-orange hair grew aggressively in seventeen different directions and his moustache alone would have earned him a fortune on the boards in old-time music hall. Graham Tidy was the dogsbody, expected to mend anything broken and to know at any given moment where everything was. He seemed young for his years and, with his round cherubic face and shy smile, he looked like a schoolboy voted the pupil most likely to succeed, the sort who always gets first prize at the end of the term –

generally a calf-bound volume of *Hymns Ancient and Modern*.

Our director, Frank Cvitanovitch reminded me, for some obscure reason, of a musk ox, that strong, phlegmatic animal who rarely makes a sound. Not that I mean to imply that Frank was taciturn, it was just that he did not believe in talking for the sake of talking, as the rest of us did, so the bulk of his conversation was confined to interrogative grunts, the odd sigh or two and an occasional 'O.K.' When, however, he decided to talk, he kept me vastly amused with his tales of his early days in Hollywood, where he had started by directing Gene Autry, the singing cowboy. When I asked him what Autry was like, Frank thought about it for a minute or so and then described him in a few biological words that left me in no doubt that he had not enjoyed that directing experience. Frank was a stocky man, whose hair was receding and leaving behind on his forehead a kiss curl, as a receding wave may leave a seashell on the shore. His meditative eyes were that attractive shade of blue that (dare I say it?) the flowers of Love-in-the-Mist attain at the height of their glory. He had undergone three heart by-pass operations, smoked like a chimney, and had just married his fifth wife. So we knew we were dealing with someone of grit, determination, strength of character and one within whose breast Hope Sprang Eternal.

The expedition's equipment – to say nothing of our personnel – had now increased to such proportions that we had to hire two more vehicles and drivers to add to our entourage. The senior one, Bruno, looked as though he would be quite happy running a stall in Petticoat Lane and doing the three-card trick on the side. With his rainbow-coloured shorts and a battered hat tilted over his magpie-bright eyes, he looked the complete Mr Fixit that he was. His second-in-command, Tiana, was a handsome, gentle boy, who gave us the impression that he had been put on earth only to ease our path through life and that our wish was his command. They were both delighted when we decorated their cars to match the Toyotas with the Trust's emblem, a white Dodo on a scarlet background.

'Now we have four Plucked Duck Trucks,' said John. 'Looks impressive.'

'Don't try to say that after a few beers,' I advised.

'What *is* this Plucked Duck thing?' asked Bob Evans.

'Well, one of the young scientists working on our project in Brazil asked us why we had a plucked duck as our emblem, as he'd never heard of the Dodo,' John explained.

'So now we have Four Plucked Duck Trucks,' I said, enunciating slowly and clearly.

'Yes, I see what you mean,' said Bob, thoughtfully. 'After a few drinks one could run into trouble saying that.'

Finally, our impatience was rewarded. All our preparations in Tana were completed and the great day dawned for our departure. The Plucked Duck Trucks were loaded up, everybody kissed everybody in sight, we ploughed our way through the host of itinerant beggars, squeezed ourselves into our vehicles and were off.

The beginning of any journey is exciting, but in this case it was doubly so, for we were to visit areas of Madagascar we had never seen before and we were in pursuit of one of the strangest animals on the planet. What more could anyone ask for?

For a time, we drove through the eroded hills that surround Tana on the central plateau. The only vegetation was Ravenala palm trees and rice paddies clustered round villages. No natural forest could be seen on either side and the hills were covered in tinder-dry yellow grass with great red gashes of erosion like sabre cuts. I was glad to see, however, that people were ploughing the rice paddies with wooden ploughs drawn by oxen, so that not only did the plough itself turn over the dark soil, but the zebu's hooves helped in the process and, of course, the zebus were manuring as they ploughed. If only more farmers would return to ploughing with oxen or shire horses and wooden ploughs, it would do the soil so much good, for this is the gentle way of turning the earth, not with the ferocious slicing of the modern plough that contributes to the death of the soil.

Presently, the road left the plateau and dropped down in a series of loops towards the sea. The road was excellent, having just been refurbished by the Chinese. It is a curious and unfortunate thing that the Chinese road-builders taught the Malagasy to eat snakes, a culinary peculiarity they had not indulged in before. The loss of these harmless constrictors will, of course, mean an explosion in the rodent population which in turn will increase the depredation of the rice crop. However, nobody looks so far ahead, biologically speaking, and this is one of the reasons why mankind is in such a mess.

This was one of the most depressing drives I have had in Madagascar. The road wound its way through miles and miles of beautiful hills which should have been covered with forest to act as watersheds, but each hillside was bare. Nothing but grass could be seen with red cicatrices of growing erosion showing glaringly. In the valleys around small villages we saw Ravenala palms, coconut palms, a few mango and lychee trees. Very occasionally, on the top of a hill we saw a pathetic little patch of original forest, like tufts of hair on the chin of a badly-shaved man. These remnants showed what the hills were clad in before the destruction. In places the raw, red earth had been cleared on such steep slopes that the soil, with no vegetation to hold it in place, had no option but to slide into the valley, causing flash floods.

To the uninitiated eye, these hills looked pleasantly green and lush but in twenty or so years they would bring disaster for those that lived amongst them and endeavoured to obtain a living from the ever-decreasing soil. With no forests acting as the lungs of the hills and holding everything together in a web of roots, the soil was simply sliding away like sand in an hourglass. How can we persuade these charming, poverty-stricken people that slash-and-burn agriculture simply edges them and ultimately their children and grandchildren nearer to starvation? Even with millions of dollars, pounds, marks and yen, it would take hundreds of years to counteract the ravages that have been perpetuated on the land and replace the forest. It seems a terrifying and insoluble problem.

As we got nearer to Tamatave, we drove through some enormous and splendid palm-nut plantations. The palm nut is a handsome tree some forty feet high with a thick, solid trunk and delicate fronds sprouting like a fountain from the top. Each trunk was protected by a thick layer of fibres and on some grew innumerable ferns, epiphytes and orchids which made each palm look as though it were wearing a massive, green fur coat. This 'clothing' must have provided a wonderful mini-jungle for a host of geckos, centipedes, frogs, spiders and so on. I wished that we had the time to stop and dissect one or two of these palms, to see what the inhabitants were. I remember once investigating a large epiphyte the size of a small bush in Guiana and, to my astonishment and delight, extracting no less than ten vertebrates from it – from tree frogs to a tree snake – and a host of invertebrates. This glorious epiphyte was in fact a teeming little city. As these epiphytes are numerous, you can imagine that the felling of one tree eliminates a dazzling array of living creatures.

At last, we arrived at Tamatave. An enormous white sand beach ran along in front of the town leading to rather murky water and, far out, as a guardian, lay a long white-ruffed reef. It was certainly an attractive beach but, apparently, the reef is breached at several points, allowing the entrance of sharks. Every country, of course, boasts that it has the worst sharks in the world, even if the last sighting was fifty years ago, but it is said that in Tamatave these beasts follow the ships into the port and those foolish enough to be lured into the warm sea have lost their limbs, if not their lives.

The houses that lined the beach were large, built in the colonial style, with wide verandas and each set well back from the road in thickly planted gardens. In many ways, it reminded me of a sort of tropical Deauville. We stayed at a large and very elegant hotel on the seafront. The veranda was as wide as a ballroom; the service was impeccable; and the view over the lush gardens to the beach and the sea and reef beyond restful to the eye.

I was delighted to find the town full of one of my favourite forms of transport, the push-push or, as it is known in other parts of the world, rickshaw. Why it is called a push-push in Madagascar I could never find out, and it was really a misnomer because it is operated more as a pull-pull. If you can imagine an upright chair with a hood (and a fringe, if you're lucky) perched up on two extra large bicycle wheels and furnished with miniature shafts, like a pony trap, that is a push-push. You take your place in the chair, the driver picks up the shafts and you are away at a gentle trot to your destination. It is an ideal means of transport: calming in its smooth, gentle progress and almost silent, moving at a safe speed or, at any rate, a speed that protects life and limb. All you hear is the faint whisper of the wheels and the soft padding of the bare feet of your driver. It does not pollute the atmosphere by noisiness or noxious smells. In these wonderful inventions you can see elegant ladies with their piles of shopping or stout business men with beetle-shiny briefcases and worried frowns being propelled to and fro, shaded from the glare and heat, cooled by the wind of their progress. Sometimes you will see a push-push simply piled high with luggage being moved from one destination to another and I once saw a four-year-old boy, immaculately outfitted and with a straw trilby perched on his glossy head, exchanging badinage with his driver so ribald that both of them were overcome with wild gusts of laughter and they almost got run down by a large, noisy and extremely smelly lorry. The impulse to hire nine of these delicious vehicles and have an Expedition Race along the seafront was almost irresistible, but reluctantly I had to discard the idea for I felt that it would distract from the high scientific profile we were trying – against the odds – to maintain.

We ate an enormous lobster for dinner which looked magnificently scarlet and regimental but appeared to have been constructed out of leather and foam rubber. In bed, we could hear the admonitory hush of the sea and the numerous nightjars calling, a strange sound like a small celluloid ball being continually dropped on a table to produce a ripple of little popping noises. It was not nearly as irritating as it sounds and was, in fact, quite soothing.

To our annoyance, the next day it was raining, but we started out despite this along the dreaded road about which we had heard so much. To begin with, it was smooth and sandy, running along the edge of the sea where huge tracts of deserted beaches stretched – not a hotel, house, tourist or beach umbrella in sight. One wondered how long it would remain like that, for they were some of the most magnificent beaches I have seen anywhere in the world, each one beautiful enough to make a developer's mouth water.

The villages we passed through were tidy, with well-built bamboo houses and thatched or corrugated-iron roofs. Each house had a neat, fenced-in area around it where the sand was carefully brushed. Some of the fences consisted of a row of quick-growing shrubs and these, together with the flowers planted, gave the villages a bright, cheerful and cared-for look. Many of the gardens had large lychee trees growing in them, the glossy, green leaves causing a dense shade, and each tree loaded with the orange-pink bunches of that delectable fruit. There were also, of course, the inevitable coconut palms, their fronds whispering like silk in the occasional breeze, their jade-green nuts fat and glossy. At one village, our caravan stopped and we purchased a couple of dozen of these huge nuts. The owner of the trees shinned up the trunks to get them and then, with his razor-sharp machete, neatly trepanned each one so that we could quench our thirst with the delicious cool liquid inside. When we had drained them dry, he took each nut, cut off a fragment to act as a spoon and then split the fruit down the middle, exposing the core of the nut like a milky white jelly, which we consumed greedily.

On the outskirts of several villages, we saw groups of children carrying fish, presumably caught by their fathers from canoes out on the reef. Some had baskets of small reef fish – a riot of crimsons, blues, glowing oranges, yellows and greens. One tiny tot was carrying a fish almost as long as she was. It was a silvery Long Tom, one of the needle fish with a protracted beak-like mouth that sticks out like a unicorn's horn. There are several different species and their sub-order rejoices in the name *Scomberesocoidei*, which sounds like a Malagasy village name. They are unnerving fish, which I had met with while snorkelling in Mauritius. You would suddenly look round and find yourself in a flock of these five foot long and dangerous-looking fish with their huge eyes and lance-like snouts. However, they were quite harmless and simply hung there in the water, watching you in the most dismal and lugubrious manner.

One small boy had a baby Hammerhead shark, black as ebony, about three feet long. These must surely be one of the most curious of all fishy creations. My first experience with a Hammerhead was when I was swimming in the beautiful bay of Trincomalee in Ceylon (now Sri Lanka). There was an area surrounded by netting to discourage the sharks from getting too intimate with you and I was floating gently along the perimeter gazing down at black sea-urchins the size of footballs, with spines as long as a carving knife, when there was a sort of disturbance like a current in the water behind me. I trod water and looked around, straight into the face of a Hammerhead some twelve feet long, who was nosing the netting in the hope of finding a way in and taking me by surprise. To be suddenly confronted at close range with that huge, incredible head and the inquisitive eyes at such close quarters gave me a considerable shock. Though I knew what they looked like, I had never seen one in the flesh and it was a macabre sight that no Hollywood horror film could ever begin to emulate. I confess it gave me such a fright that I swam rapidly for shore, even though I knew that I was safe behind the wire. I think it is the grotesqueness of the creature that inspires such alarm, as well as the knowledge that it is a fast and fierce maneater.

Looked at coolly and rationally, the Hammerhead is, of course, an amazing piece of zoological machinery. Its torpedo-shaped body forms the handle of the 'hammer', then the extraordinary head is connected to it at right angles to form the head of the hammer. In each of these outcrops is embedded an eye and beneath this is an arch-shaped mouth like a medieval church door, with a cynical droop to equal that of the late Somerset Maugham.

On my return to Jersey, I tried to find out more about this extraordinary head. It appears that the dorso-ventrally flattened shape of the head induces minimal drag when the animal is pursuing its prey. Hammerheads feed largely on squid, which are extremely fast-moving, and one species includes rays in its diet, which are even faster movers. Furthermore, the 'wings' of the head contain greatly developed olfactory and electro-receptive organs and the location of the eyes gives superior binocular vision. Another neat point is that the position of the eyes protects the shark from the flailing tentacles of a captured squid. So, in this horror-movie head, we have excellent binocular vision, excellent scent organs and a form of radar. What more can a shark need?

The road now wound its way upwards into the hills and became worse and worse. It ceased to bear any resemblance to a road and seemed rather like an ancient, dried-out river bed, where water had exposed huge carapaces of boulders the size of bathtubs and created pot-holes around them that looked as though they had been gouged out by a gigantic ice cream scoop. We all flopped from side to side like rag dolls and my hips started to complain in no uncertain manner. Although Frank drove with great skill, it was impossible to avoid bumps since the whole road looked as though it had been shelled relentlessly by an invading army and there were simply no smooth patches to alleviate the monotonous thump, shudder and bang.

The bridges that spanned the ravines and rivers did nothing to ease our passage. For the most part, they consisted of two wooden beams stretched between the banks and laid crossways on these were a series of planks. Neither the crossbeams nor the planks were new, and most of them showed signs of decay. For the most part, the planks were not fixed down and so they leapt and wobbled and banged as the vehicle passed over, with a noise like a gigantic wooden xylophone. Each car had to stop having crossed the bridge while the occupants rearranged the displaced planks for those that followed. Of course, for two vehicles to be on one of these bridges at a time would have invited catastrophe.

At one bridge, we did have an unpleasant accident which could have been infinitely nastier than it was. We had come to quite a broad river, tawny as a lion and spanned by an impressive steel bridge. Even though the cross girders were steel, laid across them were the same semi-rotting planks as the other bridges had. I was just about to teach Frank to suck eggs by telling him that if the planks gave way the art was not to get your wheels stuck between the steel girders, when that is precisely what happened. Suddenly, the planks disintegrated and the Toyota lurched over drunkenly. The steel girder started to shed bits of itself and the car sank lower and lower.

'I think Lee and I ought to vacate the car,' I said thoughtfully, opening the door.

'Coward,' said Frank.

'I don't care what sort of unpleasant things you did to the unfortunate Gene Autry,' I pointed out, 'but I am not a singing cowboy and I have a foolish preference for clinging to life for as long as possible.'

'You're deserting in the face of the enemy. You're a cad, sir,' said Frank. 'And, anyway, what about *me*?'

'You're expendable,' I said callously, climbing out on to the comparative safety of the bridge.

'Yes, we will probably direct the film much better without you,' said Lee, sweetly.

'Rats leaving a sinking Toyota,' said Frank, as the bridge gave a groan and the car sank still further. He opened his door and got out.

'I'm damned if I'm going to be the only one to go down with the ship,' he said.

On investigation, we found that the huge steel cross girders were so rusted away that they looked as if they were made of some strange variety of lace. There were places where you could stick your finger through a quarter of an inch of steel. The difficulty was that if another vehicle attempted to drive on to the bridge in a rescue attempt, in all probability it would collapse and both cars carrying all our vital equipment would plummet some seventy feet into the sleek river below. Luckily, the other Toyota and the much lighter cars had already reached the other bank. We hitched a rope to the other Toyota and slowly and very carefully it dragged its twin out and across the bridge.

With all the discomforts and hazards on the road, it was always a relief to get to a ferry, even though it slowed down our progress. The ferries were made of steel pontoons from the last World War, lashed together like giant canoes with planks on top, and propelled by a stout ferryman wielding an immensely long and thick bamboo pole. Getting on and off these ferries was quite a feat. The ferry simply edged its way to the bank or landing stage and four planks were adjusted at an acute angle. Then the driver would have to align the wheels of the vehicle on to these four planks, drive up them and land with a bang on the ferry, which would buck and sway, doing a sort of waltz in the brown waters. If the ferry was not on your side of the river, you generally had to ring a bell attached to a palm tree, and should this be lacking (as it frequently was) you had to rely on shouting yourselves hoarse until the ferryman heard you, ceased his dalliance with some voluptuous village maiden and reluctantly and slowly poled his way across to fetch you.

Once aboard the ferry, however, peace reigned. The movement was slow and smooth, the sun was pleasantly warm and the only sound was the steady plop and swish of the mammoth bamboo as it was thrust into the water by the ferryman's muscular arms. Occasionally, we would see a flight of egrets, white as stars, flying in formation to new fishing grounds, sometimes the vivid blue and russet of a pygmy kingfisher flying straight as an arrow down the river, and in the sky above us kites circled like black crosses. Now and then, we would be passed by tiny pirogues or canoes, plying the waters so gently that they made scarcely a ripple, looking like fallen leaves or seed pods as they slid silently on the river's surface.

The road afterwards got worse and worse, until we were progressing at a snail's pace, but even then we could not avoid the bone-crushing pot-holes nor the immense rocks. The road climbed so that we were several hundred feet above the sea, with an almost sheer drop down to it through coconut palms and ravenala and an almost sheer hillside above us. This had, at one time, been cleared for agriculture and then abandoned, so the low growth and vines had taken over, through which burst like a green rocket the occasional palm tree or a ravenala, spreading its fronds like a green peacock tail. The coastline was a series of huge bays with beautiful biscuit-brown beaches and occasional rocky outcrops. The sea itself was a very deep blue and where the waves broke on the brown sand they left surf in endless chains like white coral necklaces.

Eventually, we stopped at a village where we were supposed to rendezvous with Professor Roland Albignac, an old friend of ours who had created the Man and Biosphere Reserve around which we were to work. However, like most meetings in Madagascar, it did not come to pass. The local people were, as usual, helpful and full of news about our friend. He was coming by air, he was coming by car, he was coming by sea, he was here, he was there, he was in Paris and not coming at all.

Bewildered by this largesse of misinformation, we decided to have lunch at the local hotely on the offchance that Pimpernel Albignac would turn up. If he did not, we decided we would press on, for we were anxious about the next ferry which was dependent on the tide, about which we had also been given a superfluity of doubtful information.

Fortified by our simple but excellent lunch of fresh fish, chicken and the huge, obligatory bowl of rice without which no Malagasy meal is considered adequate, we pressed on. We had quite a way to go and, to our alarm, the road deteriorated still further and our progress became slower and slower, so that when we finally reached the river the sky was turning a delicate shade of green and the shadows were lengthening ominously.

To our relief, the ferry was on our side of the river, but the ferrymen were worried that the tide was going out rapidly and making the river's water-level fall. If it fell too far we could not drive off on the other side and we would be marooned on the river bed, which was not an attractive thought, as such comforts as pillows, lambas and straw mats were packed deep in the cars and it would have necessitated disembowelling our vehicles, to say nothing of food. Hastily, we drove on to the ferry – fortunately a large one which could take two cars at a time – and the ferrymen poled us speedily across the darkening river. When we got to the other side we found, to our alarm, that the tide had rushed out faster even than we expected and it was impossible for us to get off because by now the ferry was three or four feet below the landing stage. Nothing daunted, the ferrymen said they would land us on a small beach some fifty yards downriver.

To add to our joy, it had now begun to rain, not heavily, but that sort of fine rain which has a leech-like ability to penetrate everything. We reached the little sandy beach and here, to our relief, we managed to land safely. Hurriedly, the ferry turned around and went to fetch the others. We sent a message to them that we would go on to a village which lay four miles ahead and have food ready for them when they reached there. To give them additional courage, we said that we would unpack the beer. So we drove off through the drizzle, being bumped and thrown about even more now that it was dark. Our headlights were throwing all sorts of strange shadows across the road and it was impossible to tell which was a rock or pot-hole and which was caused by flickering lights.

Finally, we got to the village which was all dark and its inhabitants soundly asleep. Our arrival was greeted by a few dogs that barked in the most desultory fashion and soon returned to their beds. The hotely was a long, low, uninviting building of wood and bamboo with a thatched roof. The patron's ample wife and his family displayed no symptoms of alarm or irritation at our arrival but roused themselves from their beds with great good humour. We explained to Madame that there would ultimately be eleven of us and, as we had not eaten since noon, we were all in a mood to take up cannibalism should she not produce at once enough food to re-victual an army. She gave us a wide, placid smile, the sort of smile to give to precocious but amusing infants, and serenely drifted off to the kitchen quarters, shepherding her flock of children ahead of her.

The living-cum-dining room was large, with thick poles as cross-beams on top of which you could see the frowsty bamboo thatch. The place was furnished with long, ancient tables made out of thick untreated planks, as were the long wooden trestles. In each corner, two minute oil lamps burned, casting a faint ribbon of light that, if anything, was more unhelpful than a fire would have been. Everything had a musty, woodsmoke smell and the woodwork was faintly greasy to the touch. A few posters

Above: Antananarivo – capital of Madagascar and one of the most fascinating cities in the world. A strange conglomeration of old and new standing ankle-deep in the mushroom bed of the sprawling market.

Right: The *zoma* – the huge and magnificent market where you can buy anything from a hundred different spices, an enormous zebu hump, fish as glittering as quicksilver, flowers and fruit, while at the same time your pocket is picked deftly and elegantly.

Left: Lac Aloatra, the vanishing lake – the mountains in the background should be forest enshrouded, a water-catching shawl of vegetation. Now the lake no longer has this nourishment and is fading away.

Below: from left to right – me, John Hartley, 'Captain' Bob Evans and our nice sound recordist, Mickey Tostevin, who nearly died.

Above: A Gentle lemur looking as beguiling and tender as a film starlet, but capable of giving you a nasty bite none the less.

Below: Mihanta and I inspect a Gentle lemur in its temporary home. This animal would have ended in a stewpot but for us. As in many parts of the world, the animal is protected by law, but not in practice.

Left: One of our many abortive trips to inspect Aye-aye nests, which always turned out to be rats' nests.

Below left: The Giant Jumping rat trapline. It puzzled us that the rats walked into the traps instead of digging round them.

Right: A Giant Jumping rat looking demented, an expression which adds greatly to its charms.

Below: The wonderful Acropolis-like columns of the baobab trees, high-rise flats for so many different creatures.

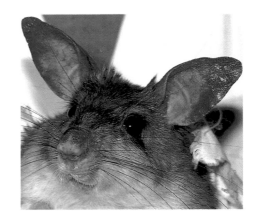

Above: Surely the Pink Panther of Madagascar: a *Fossa* lying elegantly in the branches while wondering if you're too big to eat.

Left: The sort of clearing created by the awful slash-and-burn technique for growing emerald-green rice paddies. A necessity and an evil in one.

Below: One of the bigger and more stable of the numerous ferries. If these broke down we could be delayed for days.

Above: A Malagasy chameleon. This one looks as if he gets his clothes from a colour-blind Parisian designer.

Right: Some of our team of Aye-aye hunters returning jubilantly with an Aye-aye in the bag. The first two in the pirogue are Alain and Patrice.

Below: An Aye-aye showing its huge ears and massive teeth that can demolish a coconut or your hand with equal ease.

Left: The Mauritian kestrel that we and the American Peregrine Fund brought back from the edge of extinction. There were only four known birds in the 1970s. By captive breeding, we have now increased that number: the 200th bird was recently released.

Centre: The Flat-tailed tortoise, probably one of the most handsome of the tortoise family, with its lovely shell and white moustache.

Bottom: Lee going off on an Aye-aye hunt by herself. It was unsuccessful, but she enjoyed being intrepid without my telling her not to do dangerous things.

had been nailed to the walls to give the place a 'civilized' look – a couple of bulbous blondes advertising some improbable and possibly fatal product, and an incongruous picture of the New York skyline. Apart from this, one could have been in a pre-medieval farmhouse in England under one of those Saxon kings with improbable names like Cnut and Ethelred.

Faint puffs of smoke wafted through the door that led to the kitchen, carrying a reassuring smell of food. On the tables, two cats sat folded up like pincushions in that extraordinary way that cats have. Beneath the tables lay several dogs, sleeping or voluptuously scratching their fleas, while from one corner two drowsy chickens and a duck regarded us vacantly. From behind the kitchen door, a bevy of tiny, curly-haired children, clad in tattered clothes, watched us with black eyes the size of eggcups, over-awed at this invasion of strange *vazaha* and their incomprehensible equipment. We must have looked like visitors from Mars to them.

We decided to wait dinner for the others and sent Bruno back to the ferry with encouraging messages about food and some beer to quench their thirst. In about an hour, Bruno came back and told us that the ferry had made a valiant attempt to get the last car and the Toyota across, but had been beaten by the tide. They were marooned in the centre of the river and would remain there until the tide turned.

We gave Bruno his dinner and then sent him back in case he could be of any help and to act as liaison. We decided that, as we had no means of knowing what tricks the tide might play, it was more sensible that we ate too. We had not expected a Lucullean meal, but Madame had conjured up a delicious stew of various shellfish and crabs, a big bowl of 'underground' peanuts in a hot sauce and, naturally, enough rice to stuff half a dozen pillows. We were just gluttonously wiping our plates clean with bits of bread when Bruno arrived back in a panic. The ferrymen had tried to land the Toyota too soon on the little beach. She had nose-dived off the ferry into the sand and stuck on the beach while the tide, with glee, was now coming in fast. If something were not done quickly the Toyota would disappear under water completely, carrying half of our valuable equipment. Fortunately, our Toyota had a winch on the front of her – just what was urgently needed. Bruno took our Toyota and raced back to the rescue.

They arrived exhausted: getting the vehicle out of the sand and water, heavily laden as she was, had proved a difficult task even with the winch. Without this valuable piece of machinery they would probably be there still. They sat down and wolfed their food and then set to work to unload the Toyota and see what damage had been caused by its submersion. To everyone's astonishment, relatively little had been damaged and it was not nearly as horrendous as it might have been. Unfortunately, the things that had suffered most were our precious batteries, but after each one had been taken out and dried we found that only seventy out of three hundred had been too long immersed in sea water to be of any use. Mercifully, this left us more than enough for our purposes.

The next day, it was still raining hard, which made our problem of drying everything doubly difficult. However, under the overhang of the roof, a line was rigged and our tents were draped over it, looking like whale skins. Every other bit of equipment had to be carried into the main room of the hotely and minutely inspected for damp. Wherever possible the sea water had to be washed off with fresh water. With the rain pouring down, the drying process was slow.

John discovered two more doors in the dining room and when these were opened it gave us much more light inside for examining the equipment. These three doors were rather like upright television screens so, sitting on a trestle inside, I could watch the curious happenings outside the hotely in the main street of the village. First, the lanky frame of John would pass, carrying some piece of equipment as carefully as if it was made out of glass. Then Q would pass, going in the opposite direction engaged on the same mission. Next, Bob would putter by like a clockwork toy, his hands full of sheafs of paper, his lips moving silently, a frown of concentration on his face. Then other members of the crew would appear, hoiking the dynamo or a boxful of irreplaceable batteries. Beyond this activity, groups of children stood in the rain and watched, fascinated, at what to them must have been as good as a circus.

A small, white puppy with a pot belly and an air of officiousness, with all of Madagascar to choose from and after some deliberation, came and peed copiously on one of the Toyota's wheels. Under the car itself, a group of damp, bedraggled chickens had taken shelter from the rain, while several ducks and a pig seemed to be enjoying the inclement weather, the pig rooting in the mud with small, excited grunts and squeaks and the ducks in a solemn flotilla, tails wagging, waddling, made their way down the street as if on their way to an urgent appointment. A man passed driving a small herd of zebu and, although it was obvious that both the zebu and their owner would have liked to stop and stare, they hurried on.

Presently, the rain stopped and the sun made a valiant attempt to force its way through the grey, gauzy sky. Frank unpacked his fishing rod and he and Lee made their way down to the sea, a few hundred yards away, and tried to catch our lunch, with no success. John and Q went off on a hunt and came back with a *Typhlops*, a harmless, blind, burrowing snake, black and shiny as a liquorice bootlace and about five inches long. These curious little snakes are not entirely blind but their eyes are covered by transparent scales, making it possible that the creature can only distinguish between light and dark. They live quiet, sedate lives burrowing beneath the soil and feeding on minute insects and termites. They are so secretive that practically nothing is known about their private lives.

Now the sun had come out in full force and our piles of equipment steamed quietly. Hopefully, everything would be dry on the morrow and we could continue our journey to Mananara.

6

Crystal Country and Beyond

We left early the next morning and, although it seemed impossible, the road got worse. Flurries of huge stones sent us sliding
into the very pot-holes we tried to avoid. The rain had given the
mud the consistency of red dough and embedded and hidden in
this slippery surface were sudden surprise packets of rock. My
hips and back were now so painful that I began to wish I had
taken Lee's advice and flown up to our destination instead of
undertaking this bone-shattering ride. However, the sun was
shining and the sky was blue and everything steamed gently.

We saw surprisingly few birds but plenty of other fauna. A
pair of ring-tailed mongooses with chocolate-brown faces and a
swaggering walk prudently let our caravan pass before crossing
the road slowly and nonchalantly, gazing with interest at us
from golden eyes, their tails held upright, stiff as exclamation
marks. Once, a boa crossed the road in front of us, making his
way sinuously through the mud in a series of slow loops. Reaching the other side, he paused for a rest – although he must have
been aware of our presence – before slithering up the bank and
disappearing, his body gleaming as if freshly oiled. On the whole,
I reflected, all the mammals and reptiles in Madagascar were so
tame that they were easy targets for a well-aimed machete or
the attention of even the most inadequate of marksmen.

After we had passed one village, tucked away in the folds of
the hills and almost invisible, we overtook a group of its inhabitants walking along the road, carrying something. As we got
nearer, we could see that the group consisted of men and youths,
all wearing the straw 'trilbies' so favoured by many of the

Malagasy. In their midst were four men carrying a rough stretcher on which lay the corpse of an old man, partly covered by a *lamba*. The funeral cortège seemed very merry, chatting away volubly, smoking cigarettes, waving to us as we passed, while the elderly corpse bounced and jiggled on the stretcher as if he were still alive.

The Malagasy on the whole seem to have a robust and cheerful attitude towards death. Many of the Malagasy tribes believe in exhuming from their tombs the bones of their ancestors, giving them – as it were – a good party and then re-burying them with all solemnity. It is said (with how much truth I could not discover) that in Madagascar there are taxi signs which read:

'City, 7000 francs

Marriages, funerals and exhumations, price negotiable'

The re-burial ceremony is called *famadihana* and sometimes takes place when a corpse is brought from distant parts to be incarcerated in the ancestral tomb when it also provides a chance to bring out the already-buried corpses to treat them (washing the bones, for example) and wrap them up again in a fresh silken shroud. This ritual may also be performed at the 'opening' ceremony of a new tomb, when bodies are brought to it from temporary burial sites. The *famadihana* is accompanied by much festivity, plenty of music, singing and dancing (dancing even with the ancestors' bones). On one occasion, it is reported that one of the tunes chosen was 'Roll out the Barrel'. The body is held or carried, talked to by its descendants and perhaps even taken on a quick 'walkabout' to see any new developments in the home, town or village. It is rather a joyous thing to do and so completely the opposite of our own gloomy, tear-drenched obsequies for the dead.

Finally, in the late afternoon, to our infinite relief, we reached Mananara, a conglomeration of decrepit houses that must surely have given birth to the phrase 'a one-horse town' (only in this case I think even the horse was missing). It had three roads that looked more accidental than planned, each one riddled with holes like a Gruyère cheese. The local livestock were under the

impression that this warm, pock-marked area had been constructed for their benefit. Zebu lay there, stoically chewing the
cud, treating motor traffic as if it did not exist. Two huge cockerels, with thighs like wrestlers, were having an exhilarating
fight, valiantly attempting to stab each other with long, curved,
yellow spurs. Their bronze, gold and yellow plumage shone in
the sun as they fought. In one pot-hole, a hen with five chicks
crooned to herself, looking for non-existent edible matter; in
another, four ducks, with much honking, were taking a dust
bath; in yet another, a lanky bitch in the last stages of emaciation
was lying on her side while three stalwart puppies butted at her
with their heads vigorously, in their efforts to obtain some liquid
from her shrivelled dugs.

The inhabitants of the town treated the roads, such as they
were, in the same cavalier fashion, lounging to and fro with
baskets of produce on their heads, looking neither to left nor
right, and sometimes stopping to have a gossip in what was,
after all, the main thoroughfare. Even when we blew our horns
they sometimes ignored us, or else glanced casually around and
then drifted languidly out of our way.

As befitted a one-horse town, the hotely looked vaguely like
a Wild West saloon. It was a plank-and-pole building with a
veranda running round the outside. Inside was a large bar and
eating area, with a kitchen out at the back. When you descended
from this main structure, you came upon a cluster of minute
chalets in the back garden. The beds were wooden and uncon-
taminated by such things as box-spring mattresses. The bathroom, which was slightly larger than a dropsical man's coffin,
was equipped with buckets of water and, when you had finished
your ablutions, you got rid of the bathwater by the simple
expedient of pouring it through the gaps in the plank floor. This
salubrious place was lit by one electric light bulb, little bigger
than a chestnut and dangling on the end of a frayed cord. As
the Malagasy tend to be people of small stature, the bulb was in
exactly the right position to hit me in the eye when entering or
leaving the bathroom. After I had washed my hair, the cord took
on a sinuous life of its own and wound itself loving round my
damp head in a way calculated to electrocute instantly had the

voltage pumped out by the dynamo been a shade higher. The living quarters were linked by a series of narrow paths constructed out of seashells which tinkled gently as you walked on them and, if you were late to bed, woke up everyone in the hotely.

The hotely was owned by a slim, but somewhat pugilistic-looking Malagasy who might, in his previous incarnation, have been a ruthless Mongolian pirate. It was run by his wife, a tall, slender, sumptuously beautiful Chinese lady with eyes as black and inscrutable as olives in a skin of a delicate, creamy-white shade. She was always impeccably dressed and ruled her assortment of young staff with a rod of iron. The bar, which seemed to be open twenty-four hours a day, contained a wide variety of drinks ranging from beer to a local rum which was guaranteed to grow hairs on the chest of even the most feminine of Rubens' models. Under the hawk-eyed dictatorship of Madame, meals were delicious and plentiful and served without any demur at any time of the day or night, which suited our somewhat erratic habits.

The hotely was the centre of the crystal trade and this explained a mystery to me. Madagascar and Brazil are the crystal-gathering centres of the world, Madagascar having a slight edge over the New World. In my ignorance, I had supposed that there were crystal mines somewhere on the island where muscular miners with picks extracted the precious stones from the bowels of the earth, rather like the Seven Dwarfs. Nothing could be further from the truth. The crystals, heavily disguised as stones, litter the forest floor and enterprising villagers go and collect them and sell them to local exporters, of which the hotely owner was one.

I discovered this on our first morning when I heard a curious noise. Not unlike the monotonous cry of the African tinker bird, it sounded like somebody beating tin on a tiny anvil, producing a ringing, tinkling sound that was most attractive, like a marsh full of tiny frogs in nuptial chorus. Pursuing this sound to its source, I found a group of girls sitting in the shade of a makeshift matting shelter, each armed with a small hammer, beating at large crystals, reducing them to chips the size of a Brazil nut or

91

slightly bigger. They would knock off a sizeable chunk from the mother crystal and then proceed to gently hammer it, flaking off the impurities. Each crystal thus produced glittered white and grey like a tiny icicle as it was flung on to an ever-growing heap. These were then packed up and sent to Europe to be used in the manufacture of lasers, among other things.

My discovery produced the nearest approach to animation we had seen in Frank so far, for it turned out that he collected crystals, and to find himself unexpectedly at their source was very exciting. After some hard bargaining with the owner of the hotely, who was also a crystal merchant, Frank purchased a dark crystal almost the size of the average brick and slightly thicker. It was called a black crystal, which was a misnomer, for it was a variety of smoky-greys like a Persian cat. Later on in the trip, I procured a large crystal which I considered to be infinitely superior. It was a delicate shade of pinky-mauve like well-watered red wine and was quite beautiful, even without being polished, like a gigantic, crumpled rose petal.

We settled into the hotely in a state of frustration for several reasons. First of all, we were uncertain which was the best area to set up our base camp: once this was established we had to stay put and bring any animals we caught to it, fanning out to do our hunting. Secondly, we were not quite sure which areas of forest we could hunt in without consulting the elusive Professor Roland Albignac, adviser to the Man and Biosphere Reserve which lay just outside the town, who had been meant to meet us on the way up and whose help we now needed urgently.

The whole concept of the Reserve is a fascinating and important one, particularly for a country like Madagascar which has so little forest left. The area designated for the reserve is very large and is divided up into concentric rings, rather like an archery target. The bull's-eye in the centre is a tract of untouched forest which must remain inviolate. Even scientists are forbidden entry except for the most excellent reasons and, of course, neither hunting nor tree-felling are allowed. The next ring of the Reserve is also virgin forest but it is utilized under supervision for limited hunting and tree-felling. The forest is used as it should be, gently and wisely for the service of man, but with care for the myriad other life forms that inhabit it. The third zone, the extreme outside of the target, is for agriculture, sensibly monitored so that the land is not raped, and continues to provide for the people. This is a remarkably intelligent concept and, if it works, could really help Madagascar. It was essential for us to know where these various zones began and ended so that we would know where to start our hunt for the elusive Aye-aye. So the whereabouts of Pimpernel Albignac became of great importance to us in the choosing of an area for our base camp.

I found myself in an irritating personal predicament since my hips had decided to seize up on me as a protest against the drive. I could only hobble in a fashion that made me look like an octogenarian in a sack race. My helpless condition was brought home to me rather forcibly by the sanitary arrangements in the hotely. Having made my way down the path of shells like a somnambulistic tortoise emerging reluctantly from hibernation, I had to incarcerate myself in a corrugated-iron edifice containing two cement 'footprints' and a hole, the dimensions of which made it look like an abortive attempt at the Channel Tunnel. The disadvantage of this contraption from my point of view was that, having squatted down, there was nothing with which to lever myself upright again. After the first abortive attempt when, fortunately, Lee was in earshot and could rescue me, we had to visit the toilet facilities in tandem so that Lee could prise me loose. I cannot imagine what the other inhabitants of the hotely thought we were doing, since it was hardly the place to choose for a romantic interlude.

I put the problem to Q who was, at that moment, terrorizing a local carpenter into constructing some nest boxes that we hoped, before long, would contain Aye-ayes.

'Is this carpenter of yours any good?' I asked Q.

'Yes, very good if you keep after him,' said Q.

'He doesn't leave any nails sticking through, does he? It is a favourite habit of carpenters in my experience.'

'No, he's very careful. Why?'

93

'Because when he's finished the nest boxes I want him to construct what was called, in my young days, a thunder box,' I explained.

'A thunder box? What the hell's that?' asked Q, considerably startled at my request.

'It's an invaluable open-sided box with no bottom and a hole in the top. Perch this over a hole in the ground and *voila!* you have a thunder box. Comfy to sit on and handsome as well. The one I had made in Paraguay was built out of rosewood but I can't expect those refinements here, I suppose.'

'Oh, he'll make you that easily,' said Q, 'but why are they called . . . Oh, yes, I see.'

'I'm so glad,' I said, austerely. I had no wish to go into the details of the nomenclature of this piece of furniture.

In due course, Q produced the required box. It was sturdy and well constructed and so I christened it the Bloxam Box forthwith and found my communing with nature considerably more endurable.

On our way to Mananara, we had, of course, stopped at every likely-looking village with a bit of forest left, to enquire about Aye-ayes. The results had been discouraging. Most villagers had never seen one. Even the oldest inhabitant we met, who must have been well into his eighties, vehemently denied the existence of such a dangerous beast in their midst. At one village, they did confess to having had an Aye-aye invade their plantations some ten years previously and said that it had been promptly killed. All in all, there was no account of a plethora of Aye-aye to lift our flagging spirits.

While waiting for Roland Albignac to materialize, we decided to explore the countryside, searching for a suitable site for our base camp, and to continue questioning villagers about the animal. John took one of the Toyotas and sped northwards in a hopeful way, while Q set to work to explore Mananara's surroundings. We were reasonably confident that our magic-fingered beast did exist in this area, for it was here that several had been captured a few years previously by Vincennes Zoo in Paris and Duke University in the U.S.A., to start their captive breeding programmes, which were yet to bear fruit. The youngest of the Aye-aye they caught, a baby with the unlikely name of Humphrey, had been the first Aye-aye I had ever seen and had, in effect, set our whole expedition in motion.

We had just added to our number by employing Julian, a handsome if slightly simple youth, whose claim to fame was the fact that he was an Aye-aye hunter *par excellence* and had caught several of the creatures for various zoological collections in the past. He had the audacity to shin up the trees and catch the animals by hand: no mean feat when you consider the size of the Aye-aye's teeth and the fact that it can shave off the top of a coconut – husk and shell – with a mere two or three bites. Needless to say, Julian had some impressive scars on his arms and hands to testify to the Aye-aye's biting abilities. It was decided that he and Q should go out at night to explore the forest in the vicinity of Mananara and see if they could find traces of our curious quarry. I stayed in the hotely, getting more and more irritated with the infirmities that were preventing me from joining in the night hunts as I would have wished; while Lee explored the immediate vicinity of the town.

On one of her jaunts, Lee discovered that there was a river, just on the outskirts of the town, over which a substantial iron bridge had been erected. From this bridge onwards, the road was mac-adamized and in excellent condition. It ran for about thirty-five miles and then inexplicably stopped at a small village called Sandrakatsy. On enquiry, we found out the reason for this piece of road, built in the middle of nowhere for no apparent purpose. The wife of a past president had been born in Sandrakatsy and all her ancestors had been born and buried there. If she wished to visit her ancestors from time to time (as all good Malagasy should) she had to proceed to their graves over an atrocious road. Her hus-band (as all good husbands should) became aware of her problem and solved it by macadamizing the road. Naturally, his wife was delighted and so were all the villagers who lived along the road, for it made their trips to Mananara to sell their produce that much easier. Exploring this road, Lee had found a village on the banks of the beautiful Mananara River with vast sandbanks which would make an ideal campsite. But we were still waiting on will-o'-the-wisp Roland before we could decide.

In the meantime, John returned from his scouting trip having found an area where the villagers said there were Aye-aye as well as a suitable campsite. The snag was that the road to it was appalling and the bridges geriatric. If one or more of the bridges collapsed, the whole expedition (plus any Aye-aye we may have captured) would be trapped, for unless we could use the road we were hamstrung. All we could do was wait and see what Roland had to say.

Q had been out on several night hunts with Julian and they had seen nothing. Then, one morning, while I was sitting on the veranda over breakfast, Q staggered in.

'You'll never believe it,' he said, sinking thankfully into a chair.

'Never believe what?' I asked.

'Aye-aye,' he said. 'Aye-aye everywhere. There were all dashing about in the trees. It was the most . . . well, I can't begin to describe. It was the most fabulous . . . well, it was just incredible. I mean to say . . . Aye-aye all *over* the place.'

'Now, take a deep breath and speak slowly and carefully from the diaphragm,' I said, pouring him out some coffee. Q gulped down the revitalizing fluid and told us his tale.

At about seven-thirty in the evening, he and Julian had come to an area of untouched forest. Suddenly, it seemed as if they were surrounded by Aye-aye. They saw between eight and ten animals and Q thought it must have been some sort of mating gathering. It is known that the females attract several males at a time when in oestrus. Q said that there was a lot of crashing which sounded like males seeing each other off as the females excited them. The cry that the males made was a prolonged 'ahhha' not unlike the sound of the Ring-tailed lemur, whereas the females made a shrill shriek that sounded like 'eehee'. There was also a lot of aggressive sound — hissing snorts which may, again, have been males fighting or warning each other. He saw them scuttling up and down the creepers like squirrels and licking the base of the fresh flowers of the Ravenala palm, presumably to get some sort of nectar, and chewing on a sort of gall on the trees. This they then spat out, so presumably there were some grubs or beetles which they prized within the galls. Q said they were dexterous and agile in the trees, coming down head first, climbing upside down and hanging by their back legs to feed.

Of course, this was wonderful news. It meant that we had come to the right place and located a pocket of these elusive creatures. Now all we had to do was catch them, something easier said than done. It was important that we spread the news around to the villages as well, for two days previously we had had some disquieting information from a village just down the road.

An animal collector of experience is quite used to certain amazing things that can happen. He travels far and uncomfortably in search of some beast and when he finally arrives at his destination and enquires about his quarry everyone says, 'Oh, there are none about now but you should have been here last week. I saw twenty and Charlie here ... Charlie, how many did you see? Forty. There you are, but it's the wrong season now. As I say, you should have been here last week.' An animal collector of weak moral fibre would be confined to a padded cell after a few weeks of this sort of thing. What we came up against was something worse. We had been told, in one particular village, that an Aye-aye nest had been spotted and so we went to investigate. When we got there we found that it was a rats' nest, but the villagers assured us that there were Aye-aye about for, they said proudly, ten days previously they had caught one. 'What had they done with it?' we enquired eagerly. They said that they had killed it because it was eating their coconuts. 'Had they not been informed that it was a protected animal?' we asked. They looked uneasily at each other. Yes, they had heard a rumour to that effect but they had not thought it to be true because at another village a few miles away an Aye-aye had been caught, killed and eaten. Our hearts sank, for once upon a time the Aye-aye was *fady* and, although killed, was not eaten. If it had become an item of culinary importance, the animals in the vicinity would soon be eliminated. We later found out that these two villages were within the Biosphere Reserve, which did not lift our spirits.

It was Madame's birthday that day and, in the evening, she threw a small party for us all. We put on clean shirts and shorts and I drew her a birthday card with an Aye-aye on it, only thinking afterwards that perhaps this was unwise as she may have shared the local people's belief in its malignity. However, she seemed pleased. She was dressed exquisitely for the occasion and her raven-black hair was coiffured to perfection. Indeed, she had that extraordinary 'chic' which some women carry around with them like scent.

We had a sumptuous meal, accompanied, miraculously, by champagne. To be eating so well and supping such wine in those extraordinary surroundings was a curious experience. At the end of the evening, Madame announced that on the morrow she was taking us for a picnic on an island in the nearby river. It was here, we knew, that the indefatigable Roland had released an Aye-aye he had caught and our chances of seeing it, Madame informed us, were good. As we could really do nothing sensible until the errant Roland appeared, the idea of a picnic on the river appealed to all of us, especially as we might catch a glimpse of an Aye-aye.

On the following morning, Madame left before us in a small van loaded down with comestibles and taking almost her entire staff with her. We followed on about an hour later. Opposite the island, the river was quite narrow and the colour of very strong coffee, moving sluggishly between the banks. We crossed the river in a large pirogue that was matronly in appearance and of extremely doubtful seaworthiness. When we reached the island, it turned out to be some thirty-five acres in extent, surrounded by an apron of reeds and papyrus and a botanical shambles of coffee, clove trees, coconut palms and a mass of bananas; the whole landscape was overrun by pigs and chickens.

Under one of the coconut palms there were some small huts. As I've said, the Malagasy are of small stature and build according to their needs, so most of their constructions look to our eyes like children's 'Wendy Houses' (a revolting term brought on by a surfeit of Peter Pan). Near the huts, they had assembled some comfortable Malagasy chairs that look like small 'barrel' chairs, only these are woven with fine reed. They are the most hospitable of chairs, welcoming you into their gentle embrace, but once they had engulfed your posterior you did not dare move suddenly. It was rather like being embedded in a coracle (as I once was) where any sudden shifting or an ill-timed grandiloquent gesture precipitates you sideways or, worse still, backwards, with the chair clinging to you like a burr. However, if we sat quite still in these chairs and lifted food and drink to our mouths with extreme caution, these chairs were a delight.

Once we were all installed, Madame gave instructions, like some Asian Cleopatra, and the feast commenced. There was chicken done in a heavy sauce with tomatoes, fish fried and garnished with various vegetables and the *pièce de résistance*, huge bowls of pigs' trotters, beautifully cooked, gelatinous and delicious. We had just done justice to this sumptuous array of food when who should appear from the river-bank, sauntering up in a debonair manner, but the Invisible Man, Roland himself, his big blue eyes shining, his face and partially bald head the colour of a sun-ripe pippin, his shorts and shirt immaculate.

''Allo, Gerrie,' he called cheerfully. 'I 'av come, as you see. 'Ow are zings wit' you?'

When his hand had been wrung and he had been kissed on both cheeks, he was installed in an unsafe chair and given a drink.

'Where the hell have you been?' I asked, as he beamed at me. 'From all the rumours we heard you have been everywhere from Nosy Be to Fort Dauphin.'

'I 'av been everywhere,' he said. 'Now I am adviser to the Biosphere Reserves I am 'ere, zere and everywhere at every minute. It is terrible. I am exhaust.'

Looking the relaxed picture of health and wellbeing, he refilled his glass.

'So,' he said, ''Ow 'as it been going wiz you?'

'Well, so far, so good,' I answered. 'We got the lemurs at Lake Alaotra, and at Morandava we got the tortoise and the Jumping rat. They're all safely down at Tsimbazaza. Now all we have got to do is catch those damned Aye-aye.'

'Pas de problème,' said Roland, sipping his wine. It was heartening to hear this, his favourite phrase. On a previous trip, when he had been helping us, 'pas de problème' was his answer to what seemed the most insoluble of problems which he had promptly solved for us. So frequently did he use this exclamation that we had christened him Professeur Pas de Problème and I had thus dedicated a book I had written about that trip to him. With his vibrant personality, you felt that, even if your labours were as multifarious as those of Hercules, Roland would banish them with a wave of his hand and a cry of 'pas de problème'.

'Our main problem is where to have our base camp,' I said.

''Ere,' said Roland, succinctly.

'On this island?' I asked, in astonishment.

'No, no,' said Roland, impatiently. 'I mean 'ere near Mananara, and you may hunt just outside the Biosphere Reserve. If you do not 'ave success I will get you permission to hunt in the outer ring of the reserve. I know there are Aye-aye there and that the people kill them, even though they know they should not.'

'They eat them too,' I said gloomily.

'Eat them?' said Roland, shocked. 'That is very bad. It is one thing to kill them if they eat coconuts but if they start hunting them for food, that is terrible.'

'We had thought of making a base camp at a village somewhere along that bit of macadam road,' I said. 'At least it means we can get into town for supplies.'

'Very good,' said Roland. 'That is best idea.'

'The trouble is that the TV team have so little time,' I said, 'so we must get an Aye-aye to film before they leave.'

'Pas de problème,' said Roland, soothingly. 'I 'ave already got you one.'

'You've done what?' I cried, moving incautiously. The chair

went over backwards, carrying me with it, and I lay there with my legs in the air.

'Gerrie, you 'ave to pay attention and not 'urt your 'ips,' said Roland with concern as he helped me up, dropping more aspirates than usual.

'You've really got an Aye-aye?' I asked, so astounded that I ignored the protest of my hips.

'Yes, yes, we 'ave one. You may borrow it for the film and then you give it back to me so I can release it 'ere on this island with the other one.'

I broke the good news to the team and they were delighted for, having come so far and at considerable cost, if we had not obtained an Aye-aye, it would have meant the loss of a great deal of money, to say nothing of our disappointment at not having a foot of film of one of the rarest and most bizarre creatures on earth.

'Come on,' I said. 'Let's get back to town and see it.'

'It is not docile,' warned Roland. 'It 'as not the calm disposition of 'Umphrey.'

'I don't care if it's a maneater,' I said, 'as long as we can film it.'

'I'm not insured for meeting a maneating Aye-aye,' said Frank, thoughtfully.

'That's all right,' I said. 'The Aye-aye's not insured for meeting you.'

'I don't wish to seem awkward,' said Frank, 'but I promised my new wife that I would return from this trip like a lithe, jungle animal, not a mutilated wreck.'

'We don't care if you're a mutilated wreck of a lithe jungle animal, as long as we get the film,' said Bob Evans who, for some reason best known to himself, Frank had christened Captain Bob – an appellation which seemed to suit Bob's brisk, dapper character.

'Well let's stop chuntering on about Frank's sex life and get back into town and see the animal,' I said.

'It is a big one,' said Roland.

'That's good,' I said. 'It means that even the cameraman we've got won't be able to miss it.'

Tim gave me a wounded look.

'They talk about women being gossips,' said Lee. 'For Heaven's sake, let's *go*.'

So we piled into the pirogue and went.

7

Verity the Vespertine

Along the main street from the hotely was a clapboard house up on cement pillars, which was the office of the Biosphere Reserve. Here, under the house, in the cool and the shade, reposed a large box and peering out of it, whiskers a-twitch, sat the biggest Aye-aye I had ever seen. She regarded us with mild curiosity like someone's favourite cat sitting on a windowsill. You would have thought that she had been in captivity from birth.

'I think she is old,' said Roland. 'She 'as the ambience of being old, or if not old, 'alf old.'

'Well, from the point of view of the film, it doesn't matter,' I said. 'Really, Roland, we are most grateful to you '

'Pas de problème,' said Roland.

'What are we going to call her?' asked Lee.

'Verity,' I said firmly.

'Why Verity?' asked John.

'Well, firstly, it's a fine old Victorian name. Secondly, Frank's films are famous for being "cinema verité".'

'Hum,' Frank grunted. 'You wouldn't have said that if you had seen me trying to get Gene Autry on to a horse.'

'Nevertheless, Verity she shall be,' I said, and Verity she remained, even when we discovered that she was a he.

Now that Professeur Pas de Problème had arrived in our midst we could galvanize ourselves into some sort of activity. As always in Madagascar, the first thing we had to do was to go and see the president of the whole Mananara region. He was

103

a pleasant, quiet personality who, with typical Malagasy good manners, almost concealed his secret thought that we were all eccentric in the extreme, perhaps bordering upon madness. Since we appeared benignly deranged, he was content that we should invade his area of jurisdiction and welcomed us with charm.

Having made our mark with the higher echelon, we travelled the macadam, ancestor road until we came to the village of Antanambaobe, which is where Lee had spotted an area which might serve us as a camp site. Along the road, of course, one gave up any hope of seeing real forest and had to try to enjoy what man had made of it. It had a curious charm. There was a bright-green lushness about it, with Ravenala spreading their fans and, in the tiny ravines where erosion had cuddled a pocket of mud, suddenly a tiny paddy field, square like an emerald-green pot spilt from a child's watercolour paint box. In the villages with their neat gardens the lychee trees were orange-red with fruit and the clove trees were such perfectly elongated egg-shapes that they looked like fairytale efforts at topiary.

As we drove along, we got all the scents of sunlight on leaves, the rich plum-cake smell of earth and rotting vegetation until, suddenly, we were in a village. Immediately, we were enveloped in delicious aromas – coffee, cloves, vanilla – each seed of these aromatic plants laid out carefully on reed mats to dry in the sun and fill the air with a magical mixture of perfume.

Antanambaobe was a large village of some thousand souls, but it did not seem intrusive, for the village lay so scattered among the coconut and clove plantations that, except for the string of houses along the road, we were unaware of such a large conglomeration of human beings. Here, we met the *délégué* of the region. These are government appointees, not necessarily from the region, and generally (as we soon found out) at odds with the locals. From the point of view of the locals they have two black marks against them: they are not local and they are government personnel.

Our particular *délégué* was called Jerome – a man whose smile made you feel instinctively for the safety of your wallet. He was obviously delighted at the thought that we had chosen 'his' village and his eyes rambled appraisingly and delightedly over our well-loaded vehicles.

He had a broad and ready grin which, like most Malagasy, displayed a mass of huge rotting teeth. Any dentist paying a visit to this beautiful island would either have a nightmarish time surrounded on all sides by these disintegrating fangs or would decide to take up residence and make himself a fortune. After the beautiful, solid white teeth of Africans, gleaming like Italian tombstones, this Malagasy display of stalagmite and stalactite dentures in shades of black, yellow and green comes as something of a shock. Jerome, however, was different, for in the forefront of his mouth, positioned carefully among the crouched rotting stumps, was a gold tooth shining like a sun in a stormy sky. The person responsible for this adornment to his face appeared to have been either an amateur, or so overwhelmed with the importance of handling this fortune that he had planted it awkwardly so that the tip peeped coyly over Jerome's lower lip.

Instantly, we christened him Snaggletooth, but never used this unbecoming sobriquet to his face, always calling him Monsieur Jerome with a reverence that seemed to surprise him. We did not, we said, wish to disrupt village life more than we had to and, therefore, we would like to camp on the sandbanks down by the river. We needed some shade, not only for ourselves but for the living quarters we intended (with his help) to erect so that we were self-sufficient. Then we went down to survey the area.

We were greatly cheered because while we were discussing the pros and cons of the site a large, glistening snake made a sinuous appearance from out of the bushes and slipped, as slowly and seductively as a Balinese dancer, right across the area we had decided on. Q caught it and we all let its lovely, warm, dry length, smooth as silk, slide through our hands like water coloured green and brown with a hint of gold. We let him go and wished him well on his journeyings. Not being a superstitious crowd, we decided that this was a good omen.

The site was certainly very beautiful, with the broad, brown river moving at a stately speed between rocky and sandy dunes. The opposite shore looked to the uninitiated eye like thick, untouched forest, but this effect was produced by a few large old trees that – by some miracle – had been left standing. Around their massive trunks small growth had sped upwards to twenty or so feet in height, and from this erupted groups of smaller trees, coconut palms and the inevitable Ravenala.

Carefully, we paced out and marked the area which would be our communal dining-sitting-room-kitchen, and another area on which the animal shelter was to be erected. By now, Snaggle-tooth had a cohort of villagers around him, all giving expert advice and telling him how the thing should be done and he was getting more and more irritated, his gold tooth flashing like a dagger in the sun as he endeavoured to retain his leadership over what was, after all, a cataclysmic event in the history of the village. Never before in recorded history had no fewer than nine *vazahas* taken up residence in Antamambaobe, bringing with them four cars, each stuffed to the gills with unimaginable treasures. Moreover, it was well known to all that *vazahas* were stupid and that money fell from them like leaves from the trees if they were shaken properly. We were assured by a chorus of eager voices that the bamboos for the supports and the palm fronds for the roofs would be ready first thing in the morning and that building would commence the moment we arrived. I wanted us to be there when work started, to make sure we were not enthusiastically given a triangular building when we had asked for a square one. Such things happen, not only in the tropics, but in Europe as well, as I have found out to my cost. I have friends who, building a house in Greece, left everything in the hands of their builder and, on their return, were horrified to find the house facing away from the entrancing view that had made them want to build there in the first place. The excuse given was that the winds in winter blew from the view to the house. When it was pointed out to the builder that my friends were not there in winter, so did not care about the winds, he looked crestfallen and burst into tears. It had taken a lot of ouzo to heal the wound to his *amour propre* and I did not want to have such an experience happen to us in Antanambaobe.

I also enquired into the peregrinations of the local zebu herds, as I had no wish to step out of my tent of a morning to find that twenty or thirty large zebu had left calling cards as big as soup tureens, the size and consistency of which would bear testimony to their splendid health and the magnificent state of their bowels. After this, we repaired to the road, where we repeated all our instructions yet again. Jerome spent his time listening to this repetition with great attention, nodding his head in agreement while picking his nose voluptuously, presumably to aid concentration. Finally, we were ready to go and he removed his forefinger from its profound and comprehensive archaeological excavations and, beaming with goodwill, shook hands all round. I noticed that I was not the only member of our party to surreptitiously wipe my hand on my shorts.

When we drove back to the hotely the sky was the palest and softest blue. Then, suddenly, it was invaded by battalions of cauliflower-shaped, belligerent-looking, dark grey clouds. They extinguished the sun as if blowing out a candle, bustled the blue away and opened their copious bosoms to feed us rain. No one who has not been to the tropics can imagine the fierceness and suddenness of a tropical downpour. When we reached the hotely the thrumming of the rain on the roof and the palm fronds made speech almost impossible. I saw a beautiful scarlet and black butterfly take refuge under a leaf and then, as the rain increased in volume and its leaf began to bend and shake, it decided that it had chosen unwisely and attempted to fly to a more protected spot. Immediately, it was pelted to the ground by the raindrops and within seconds its body was mashed into the ground before I could rescue it. In this sort of rain, the drops beating on your head and face become almost painful. The roar of the water hitting the palm fronds was like the sound of a giant waterfall. The road disintegrated, turning within seconds from candy pink to an almost scarlet sludge. Raindrops the size of twenty-nine carat diamonds (but much more beautiful) dripped from the curves of the corrugated-iron roof. The temperature dropped ten degrees. Then, suddenly, the clouds moved majestically away, the sun emerged rather shamefacedly and everything started to steam gently, like a kettle summoning up the lung power to boil.

That night, Lee fed Verity on a curious diet that we had evolved. Firstly, there were beetle larvae, some three inches long and weighing almost an ounce. They looked like some curious living eiderdown as they waddled about like fat old ladies in pale silk nightgowns and would, presumably, turn into the large beetles we had seen, each the size of a matchbox, gleaming black and brown as if newly polished and with huge rhinoceros-like horns on their heads. The larvae, I must confess, were rather revolting, like maggots viewed through a high-powered microscope, but Verity had no such artistic qualms and fell on them with all the enthusiasm of a child presented with an ice cream. He also ate bread balls made of raw egg and honey, which he loved. In addition, for we did not want his teeth to overgrow, he had sticks of sugar cane and the occasional coconut. On this diet, he thrived and within a few days was coming down to the wire to take food from Lee's hand.

When we got back from organizing our camp site, Julian said he wanted to go off night hunting on his own to see if he could find any signs of our quarry around the Antanambaobe area. We let him go, hoping that he would return in the morning to tell us that we were pitching camp in the largest concentration of Aye-ayes known to science, but rather doubting it. The main trouble with Aye-ayes is the fact that they are like gypsies, forever moving on. They will find a suitable farm to plunder and, then, when they have eaten their fill, they will make a nest to sleep in. These are architecturally rather bulky edifices of leaves and vine, with soft bedding inside. In these bowers they would rest up during the day and sally forth at night, like pirates, seeking another farm to decimate. It was only by climbing up to these nests in the daytime that you stood any chance of a capture. The annoying thing was that the local rats built nests of somewhat similar size and design and you could not tell whose abode it was until you had climbed up to it. To have to climb fifty or sixty feet up a tree (a hazardous task in itself) only to find that the nest belonged to a rat was extremely irritating and time-wasting. It appeared – although we were not wholly certain of this – that the Aye-aye built its nest, slept in it, and the next day moved on to build another nest for the following night. So even if you had, with extreme difficulty, climbed up to a nest, you might well find it empty. Another factor was that we had arrived in what was thought to be the middle of the breeding season and, because we know so little about the Aye-aye, we do not know if the mother remains in the same nest after the baby is born, until it is old enough to follow her, or whether she continues her normal foraging and builds a new nest each night, transferring the helpless young to this nursery.

Our lack of knowledge of this incredible animal (as, indeed, most animals) is lamentable. However, there is hope. Some years ago, a few Aye-aye were caught (at the time, they were thought to be the last ones in existence) and transferred to an island called Nosy Mangabe, which was a sanctuary. Here they flourished and to this island came a redoubtable lady called Eleanor Stirling. She has been studying these island Aye-ayes for two years now and, when she finally publishes her Ph.D. on them, it is to be hoped that most of the animal's secrets will be revealed.

The next morning Julian appeared, totally unconcerned, grinning happily, to report that his mission had been unsuccessful. Although we had expected it, this was still irritating news and so we set off for the campsite in a gloomy mood. Our spirits lifted, however, when we reached the river-bank to find that everything we had asked for had been done, a near miracle anywhere in the world. The giant bamboos, each the circumference of a saucer, green and old-ivory yellow, with black markings like paint strokes here and there, had been cut on the opposite side of the river and then floated across. Piled up, they looked like a collection of giant sticks of barley sugar. Bamboos are one of Nature's most astonishingly useful varieties of plant life. Cut off one of their joints (each measuring perhaps three feet in length) and then remove one end and you have an almost unbreakable and elegant receptacle: a jug, a jar, a water carrier or a vase. Cut the whole joint in half, trim it, and you have two mugs; split it lengthways and you have a giant ash tray or a convenient, tray-like object for keeping such things as paperclips, pens and pencils in.

We had measured out the kitchen-living area and work commenced as soon as we arrived. It was fascinating to watch the building take shape. Firstly, the holes for the uprights were dug with spades. The only other tool to be used for construction was a coup-coup (known in different parts of the world as a machete, cutlass, parang, kri or yataghan). Shaped something like a young brother to a sabre and razor sharp, this invaluable tool becomes, in the hand of a skilled man, almost part of his body, a deadly and accurate elongation of his arm. A well-honed coup-coup can slice off a man's arm, split his skull in two, or delicately bisect a grass blade.

The speed and accuracy with which the villagers used these deadly weapons was incredible. As soon as the holes were ready, the bamboo lengths were shaved of any leaves or small branches. The bamboo was then lowered into the hole, so we could judge the height because we did not want a house built which, while eminently suitable for the Seven Dwarfs (or Malagasy), would have had us constantly banging our heads on the rafters, as if we were living in an Elizabethan cottage. Once the height of the building was established, the top end of the bamboo was cut into the shape of a V, planted in the hole and well tamped down. Meanwhile, one of the giant bamboos had been carefully skinned of its tough bark, which provided the necessary 'rope' to bind the cross beams to the uprights. While this was being done, the roofing was being prepared. This consisted of palm fronds whose central rib had been sliced half through, so that the fronds on each side of the leaf could hang together, tent fashion. When the rafters of the house were in place and tied, this roofing of fronds was hauled up, placed along the beam and fastened in place.

By lunchtime, the basic structure was up and half the roof was on. The speed was incredible. By the time we returned from lunch, the structure was ready. By teatime, the tents were up, ours under a breadfruit tree, while the team preferred to erect their smart green ones in a regimented line. Frank insisted on perching his orange-and-white-striped tent up on a sandbank, which completely ruined the view from our tent. But who were we to argue with the director? Now only a few details were needed to complete the layout – latrines, a rubbish hole and so on. Our multifarious equipment was unloaded and stacked haphazardly in our newly-erected house to be sorted. By this time, as far as the village was concerned, the circus had come to town.

While frenzied activity was taking place a little way up the hill, where the animal house was in the process of construction, what appeared to be the entire younger population of Antanambaobe descended on us and ringed us in a circle twelve deep around the house. They were very handsome, very quiet and orderly but, as the news of our eccentricities spread, more and more children arrived and the ring steadily got closer and closer. They *were* exceedingly well behaved, but the mere fact that they all sat around us prevented us from sorting out our goods and chattels and getting settled in. Apart from this, the temperature inside our living-quarters rose by five degrees simply from the heat given off by the massed bodies.

Of course, as far as the kids were concerned, we were something out of this world. If we had arrived by flying saucer, we could not have made a greater impression. We were a combination of Barnum and Bailey's Circus, the Lord Mayor's Show, the Changing of the Guard, with several Walt Disney films thrown in. It was interesting to see their faces, wide-eyed, watching us with the avidity of tele-addicts. Most of the gear we unpacked was as incomprehensible to them as the equipment 007 was always using in the Bond films. Only when we produced things they understood would their eyes widen and sibilant whispers of recognition would rustle among them; clothing, *lambas*, tins of sardines and corned beef, gleaming golden bottles of cooking oil, rice and tins of biscuits. Our every move was scrutinized as closely as if they were Scotland Yard on the scene of a crime. We did nothing that was not recorded by their shining mulberry eyes, no doubt to be divulged to their eager parents

111

that evening. I watched them, stepping over, tripping over and occasionally by mistake stamping on children.

'I've no wish to be a spoilsport to these kids,' I said to Lee. 'This is obviously the biggest event that has ever occurred in their short lives. But if they would move further back so we are not suffocated, it would be a help. It would be an even greater help if they went away and came back tomorrow, if someone could persuade them that we are here for several weeks and will not vanish overnight. Can you go and track down Monsieur Jerome and see what he can do? Make sure that he knows we *love* the kids, but not at this precise juncture.'

We were in the process of drinking – with ill-concealed expressions of disgust – smoky, very bitter, stewed tea, laced with sweetened condensed milk, when Lee returned from her errand, giggling.

'What's up?' I asked. 'Did you see Monsieur Jerome?'

'Yes,' said Lee, 'and he quite understood, so he suggests we have visiting hours.'

'We have *what*?' enquired John, incredulously.

'Visiting hours.'

'You mean, like a zoo?' I asked.

'Well, yes, I suppose so,' said my wife.

'The wheel has turned full circle,' said Frank with relish. 'I knew you'd end up in a zoo.'

'I still don't understand,' I said.

'We have certain hours when they can come and look at us,' Lee explained. 'I suggested between half eleven and half twelve. I thought we'd be eating then and so they wouldn't get in the way so much.'

'And?'

'He said they'd be in school then. So finally we settled on four o'clock to five-thirty,' said Lee. 'It seemed the best all round.'

'Yes, it's almost a matinee,' said Captain Bob, adding wistfully, 'I used to go to a lot of matinees in my youth.'

'What are we supposed to do for them?' I asked.

'Nothing,' said Lee, 'just behave naturally.'

'We can't do *nothing* with an audience eight hundred strong,' I protested. 'We must do *something*.'

'Yes,' said Mickey, his red hair coiling in all directions, his moustache bristling with enthusiasm. 'We must. I can sing some old music-hall songs for them. You know, "Any Old Iron", that sort of thing.'

'I can accompany you with comb and paper, if I can find my comb,' said Tim.

'I can do the dagger scene out of *Macbeth*,' I said. 'I used to be a pretty fearsome Macbeth.'

'You're pretty fearsome *without* being Macbeth,' Frank observed.

'Lee can sing in French,' I said, ignoring him. 'She's got a lovely voice.'

'So can I,' said John eagerly. 'I can sing.'

'No, you can't,' I said firmly. 'Having known you for thirty years and having heard you doing what you call singing in a host of different places around the world, I can say unequivocally, that you can't sing. You can't carry a tune and you can't remember the words.'

'Is that true?' asked Graham, interested. 'I can't either. Perhaps we could do a duet?'

'God forbid. You'll frighten the lives out of the poor little things. In Sierra Leone they used to call John "Masa who get pain for belly".'

Alas, our high hopes were in vain. At four o'clock, we looked out eagerly for our audience but no one arrived. We discovered later that the parents had given the children such a telling-off for their unseemly behaviour that the poor kids were frightened to come down. In addition, when we went up to where the cars were parked on the road, we found a large notice in rather uncertain capitals, nailed to a post. It said, in Malagasy, 'The *vazaha* are our honoured guests. They must not be worried. They can be looked at in the evening by a few people at a time.' It was obvious that the village was going to respect our privacy at the cost of our thespian ambitions.

In spite of this, our campsite was quite lively, for it lay betwixt two paths that led from the village to the river. One path went down to where a highly unseaworthy pirogue was moored to ferry people and their goods and chattels across the chocolate-coloured waters. The other path meandered down to the river's edge where the ladies of the village made pilgrimages twice a day to get water and to do their washing-up. As, for the most part, I was crippled and confined to camp, these two paths, anthropologically speaking, provided me with a lot of pleasure and interest.

There was, for instance, the handsome young man who lived somewhere on the opposite bank. He possessed a fine, fat, chestnut-coloured zebu, a rich possession for so young a person and one of which his ancestors were undoubtedly proud. Twice a day, he would bring this handsome animal down for a bathe. At these times, should the ferryman be on our side of the water, he would unhitch his pirogue, paddle across and make fast to a large root on the other side. The zebu, now up to its shoulders, would be thoroughly scrubbed down by its owner with a handful of coarse grass and sometimes a flat stone, a process which the zebu revelled in. Whilst making sure that every inch of his prize was scrubbed meticulously to remove all fleas, ticks, leeches, dandruff and other things zebu are prone to, the incredulous zebu man would be regaled by the ferryman as to the latest goings on in the totally mad *vazahas'* camp. The night we tested the generator and floodlit the camp with a fearsome light, the ferryman, in his efforts to describe it to the sceptical zebu man next day used such grandiloquent gestures that he overturned the pirogue and ended up, spluttering, in the river. The zebu, I was glad to see, viewed his new bathing companion benignly.

During these bovine washing sessions, the zebu man would get so engrossed in the ferryman's graphic tales that he would cease operations on his charge. He eagerly questioned the ferryman and meanwhile the zebu would get bored. It would haul its glistening bulk out of the water and go wandering along the bank, trailing its tether behind it. Presently, it would disappear among the trees and in a minute or so uproar would break out as some farmer found it browsing placidly on his crops. The zebu man would then have to run after it, catch it, exchange a brisk volley of insults with the enraged farmer and hurry back to that bewitching fairytale teller, the ferryman.

Down the other path, the ladies would come, bright as parrots in their gay *lambas*, carrying piles of pots on their heads to wash. Some were tin bowls with most of the enamel worn off and some were plastic whose garishness had dimmed and whose surface had acquired a sort of fur. This deterioration was not to be wondered at when you saw the method employed to clean them, ingenious though it was. A pot would be plunged into the river and a generous handful of sand would then be placed in it. This would be carefully positioned by the feet. While one foot held it so that it was not swept away by the current and turned it round and round, the toes of the other foot were busy sanding down, as it were, the interior of the bowl. This, of course, left the hands free for gesticulation or for the purpose of aiding the mastication of fearsome lengths of sugar cane, ripping it to pieces with an ease that an Aye-aye might have envied. Each time the ladies passed and re-passed us they would peep at us shyly from under the leaning tower of Pisa of pots on their heads and greet us in gentle, soft voices, like the cooing of doves. They were enchanting and I deeply regretted not knowing Malagasy, for I would have loved to hobble down to the river's edge and gossip with them as they dexterously twirled their pots with their toes, making a soothing, slushing noise like a Lilliputian steam engine, so much nicer than a washing machine.

There was a man whose behaviour puzzled us all. We had many arguments as to what the meaning of it was, but we were too cowardly to go and ask him. He would cross the river by the pirogue, and then make his way across the sand dunes to the washing-up path. He was minuscule and slender, carefully dressed in shorts and a clean shirt. On his head was perched the straw trilby so beloved of the Malagasy and he had a stick across his shoulder from which dangled a small straw bag, presumably containing his lunch. As he came opposite our living-quarters, he would stop, doff his headgear, duck his head in an embryonic bow and mumble a greeting, to which we would reply. This ceremony over, he would replace his hat and continue up the path past the animal house. It was only when he had done this several times that I noticed what he was doing. Having raised his hat to us, he would then raise it again as he passed the animal house, whose sole occupant was Verity. Did he think this animal was malignant and that it behove him, therefore, to show it courtesy lest he was overtaken by some terrible misfortune? We shall never know, but each time he crossed the river he doffed his hat to both us and our prized possession.

Another character who became well known to us was the Girl with the Bucket. Plump but graceful, with a wide, glittering smile and sleepy, provocative eyes, this young lady would come down to the river to fetch water twice a day. For this purpose she had an immense yellow plastic bucket. We would hear her singing to herself, rich and liquid as a blackbird, and then she would appear wearing the bucket over her head like a hat. As the bucket was so huge, it enveloped her head completely, so that all she could see were her feet, yet she made her way down the path, with all its rocks and roots, as sure-footedly as a chamois. The bucket, of course, acted like an amplifier, enhancing her song with an echoing quality. On her return, balancing the bucket of water the right way up on her head, she would give us her dazzling smile, bid us good day and continue up the hill, still singing happily. We used to greatly look forward to her all too brief serenades and her circus act with the bucket.

By now, Verity had become very tame and each evening Lee would go and feed him by hand. Feeding by hand is not strictly necessary but does help to give you an accurate idea of how much food the animal is taking. Left to themselves, animals tend to throw food about and trample it to bits so that when you clean out the cage in the morning it is extremely difficult to find out what its intake has been. Verity loved his honey balls, each the size of a ping-pong ball, with their nutritious contents of honey, egg and bread. Then he would have his revolting, fat, beetle grubs, which he scrunched up with relish. As an Aye-aye's massive teeth are constantly growing, it is essential for the animal to have something hard to gnaw on, to prevent its teeth from turning into tusks. The answer, of course, was lots of rotting logs, coconuts in their husks and sticks of sugar cane. These and the beetle grubs were provided by Marc, who had been foreman on our building work, a short, stocky, cheerful figure, who became deeply devoted to Lee, but would insist on calling her 'Mama', to her annoyance.

It was fascinating to watch Verity's various methods of approach to each foodstuff. The honey balls were soft and so he used his middle finger like a fork to carry bits to its mouth. The same treatment was meted out to the fat grubs, but he generally bit their heads off as a preliminary, so they writhed there, disgorging various parts of their internal organs and deflating like rather repulsive balloons. The sugar cane he bit into between the joints with his enormous teeth, stripping away the tough outside skin until he could get at the softer, juicy pith inside. When each piece of sugar cane had been treated in this way, they looked like weird medieval instruments, a curious sort of basset horn, perhaps, or some kind of archaic flute.

The coconut (almost as large as he was) presented different problems. First, the thick, shiny, green husk had to be torn away with his chisel-like teeth. When he judged that enough had been removed for his purpose, he could start work on the nut, now partially exposed. He went through this like a circular saw, producing a hole about two and a half inches in diameter. These, of course, were young nuts with the 'milk' still in them – so Verity once again used his finger, dipping it through the hole into the liquid and then bringing it to his mouth with incredible speed and dexterity. At this stage of its development, the meat of the coconut has not congealed as in the nuts we get in Europe. It is like a semi-transparent whitish jelly, faintly sweet and with a coconut flavour. Having exposed this delicacy, Verity would now use his versatile digit – the magic finger – to hook the jelly out with great rapidity. When he had obtained all the jelly he could reach, there was a pause while the hole was enlarged and then his finger came into play again. This third finger is not longer than normal, but it looks it because it is so attenuated and bony.

When given a rotten log, he would inspect it carefully, whiskers a-quiver, ears turning to catch the faintest whisper of a fat grub gnawing in the interior of the wood. Then he would attack the log with his teeth to expose the tunnel, insert the finger as delicately as a surgeon's probe, spike the grub on the nail and deftly pull it from its subterranean home. Madagascar, curiously enough, has no woodpeckers and it has been suggested that the Aye-aye takes the role of the bird in the ecological framework of the forest.

The only sound he made – if he was suddenly disturbed – was a loud sniff. Q described it perfectly as sounding like someone trying to stifle a gigantic sneeze. One night, Mickey heard him calling, a sound rather like a love-sick cat, and such was his devotion to duty that he got out his equipment, crept up to the animal house and recorded him, facing the attacks of a million joyful and hungry mosquitoes. From watching Verity and others of his kind, I got the very strong impression that they were tough animals, survivors if you like, and possessed of a greater intelligence than other lemurs I had hitherto come into contact with.

Settling into camp proved to be a process as complex as moving into a new house. Anguished cries from one or other of us demanding to know the whereabouts of anything from a screw to a tin of sardines, a compass to a bottle of beer, were always answered by Graham's placid voice. By some sixth sense, like water-divining as yet unexplained by science, Graham had imprinted on his mind a sort of map of our possessions which, computer-like, he could track down. Once, in a casual way, I wondered where Lee had got to. Without even looking up from the book he was reading, he gave me a quick run-down of her activities since she had risen that morning, ending up with the information that she had just gone up to the village for a moment, probably to see about sugar cane. Graham was a sort of expedition replica of Jeeves and without him we all became as disorientated as a Pavlovian dog with no bell.

Meanwhile, the hunts continued, with John, Q and Julian going out nearly every night and coming back empty-handed. Once, they spotted an Aye-aye and Julian, with his incredible speed and agility, shinned up the tree and caught the animal by the tail. Not surprisingly, affronted by this indignity, the Aye-aye turned and sank its incredible teeth into Julian's hand. Luckily, before it could really get down to amputation, Julian let go, but it still left its mark. Needless to say, when they got back, the camp resounded with cries, 'Graham, where's the sticking plaster?'; 'Graham, where's the tube of antibiotic ointment?' Graham's soothing voice would direct our endeavours like a Harley Street specialist.

Camp routine was now getting under way. Marc came every day, bringing coconuts and sugar cane for Verity. Children came in wide-eyed, timid groups bringing obese beetle grubs, and we employed two buxom girls from the village to bring us water, wash up and wash our clothes. For some reason, cooking became a team affair. Captain Bob, we discovered, had a magical way with rice, producing it *al dente* with great skill. We also sent him into Mananara to do shopping, for we discovered that the Captain was not only King Rice but had an extraordinary instinct for finding things in that one-horse town, with its tiny sprinkling of emporia. Like a magician, he would unearth the most bizarre foodstuffs from the most unlikely little food shops. He would set off cheerfully with our list and generally, to our surprise, return with everything we had asked for. Frank and I hatched a plot that one day we were going to give him a list containing things like caviar and quails' eggs and see what happened. We never did, however, I think partly out of a vague fear that he would produce them. We did suggest that he changed his name by deed poll to Mr Fortnum Mason, an idea which, for some churlish reason, he would not agree to adopt.

Tim, we discovered, before taking up the gentle art of cine photography, was planning to be a chef and take the taste buds of the world by storm. In a misguided moment, he implied that he considered desserts to be his natural forte. Immediately, a clamour for exotic desserts arose on all sides. Suggestions ranging from treacle tart to profiteroles came from us. Deftly, like a skilful matador, he simply avoided our greedy attack by saying he could and, indeed, would have produced all these delicacies, including Spotted Dick and Roly-poly Pudding, but where were the ingredients? He was told that we had bananas and sugar and condensed milk, that if he could not produce something with these humble ingredients he had no right to claim any gastronomic virtues and that, in fact, we would consider that our suspicions that he had never seen the inside of a kitchen — and, even if pressed, would have extreme difficulty in boiling water — would be justified. Stung by our comprehensive execrations, he attacked the bananas, the sugar and the milk and, to our delighted astonishment, proceeded to conjure from these unlikely ingredients more different, delicious desserts than I would have believed possible.

For some reason (probably in a weak moment we had implied that we liked cooking), Frank and I were given the main dish to conjure up. Corned beef and sardines on rice did not meet with the hushed reverence that we had hoped for. Sardines on toast, followed by corned beef fritters, were treated in an extremely uncouth manner. Curried corned beef with sardines failed lamentably to meet with the cries of joy that our cooking normally evoked. I was forced to agree with Frank's assessment of the situation, that we were dealing with a bunch of untutored, uncivilized louts, who could not distinguish between a carrot seed and a crêpe suzette.

Frank took unfair advantage of me by slipping into town and cornering the market on some fresh zebu meat. Normally, this delicacy has all the dietetic appeal of the sole of a shoe of a foot soldier in Napoleon's army, but Frank lived up to his middle European ancestry and, by some miraculous means, produced a delicious goulash containing beautifully tender meat. Determined not to be outdone, I paid a visit to the market to see if I could find something to titillate the palates of the team with. Lying on the floor in one corner — everything was on the floor in this market — were some very curious items which attracted my attention. They looked, at first glance, like Victorian Easter bonnets in pink and grey with long ribbons attached. When I say Easter bonnets, of course, I am being charitable. They looked like Easter bonnets that had never had the benefit of soap and water, that had been run over a number of times by an exceedingly heavy steamroller, buried in a rich and fragrant compost heap for several months and then disinterred to take their place as a food item in the market. Close and detailed inspection of these strange artifacts led me to the conclusion that they were, in fact, octopus to which something terrible had happened, so that they no longer resembled the shy-eyed, glossy octopus I had been used to from my childhood. They looked, in fact, as though, if you accidentally hit someone over the head with one, it would not only fracture their skull but cause possibly fatal brain damage. However, my curiosity has always been easy to arouse and I work on the principle that you should always try everything once, so I bought two of these mummified cephalopods and took them back to camp.

Here, in the utmost secrecy, I showed them to Frank. When he had recovered from the shock I asked him how he thought they ought to be prepared.

'We must resuscitate them,' he said, after some thought.

'Not me,' I said firmly. 'I'm not giving mouth to mouth resuscitation to an octopus that has been dead for two hundred years.'

'No, no. I mean soak them in water,' said Frank. 'They're dehydrated. They need rehydration.'

So we put them in a bowl of water. If anything, they looked slightly more macabre than before. We left them for a couple of hours and then peeped at them. To our astonishment, they had absorbed a lot of water and were beginning to bear a faint resemblance to the octopus we knew and loved. By evening, they were beginning to look quite plump, slimy and friendly. We chopped them up into small chunks, basted them in oil, added every condiment at our disposal, together with a handful of the hot, delicious, aromatic, Malagasy black pepper and set them to simmer, hoping that by suppertime everyone, exhausted and hungry from their day's labours, would fall on this with rapture. This was not quite what happened but everyone agreed that the final result was edible – if a bit on the chewy side. I said the roughage was good for the digestion and the chewiness good for the teeth.

'Yes, bungs you up and extracts your teeth at the same time,' said Frank.

One day, there was great jubilation because Captain Bob returned from town with a bundle of chickens. When the feathers were off they were a disappointment. They were those strange, Malagasy fowls that look like long-legged Old English fighting cocks, magnificently coloured and with eyes as fierce as a cockatrice, but remove their plumage and you find they have practically no breast, and thighs like a ballet dancer suffering from anorexia. Whatever loving culinary care we lavished on them made no difference, they simply became tougher and tougher.

One of these enormous, glittering birds, strutting like a belligerent avian pearly king, used to come down from the village each morning with a harem of drab hens. Our tent had been pitched right in the middle of his territory, a situation that he viewed with much disapproval. As the mist lifted off the river and the coucals started their beautiful, burbling, liquid calls, this great cockerel would come swaggering up to the entrance of the tent and fix us with his fierce golden eyes, his head twitching to and fro as he viewed us with first one eye and then the other, apparently finding us equally obnoxious from either optic. Then he would throw back his head and give a prolonged, harsh and unmusical crow. Having, he felt, intimidated us into submission, he would enter the tent and start scratching about among our possessions with his huge feet, for he was convinced that most of our equipment was edible. A well-aimed shoe would soon disabuse him of this and he would stalk out with offended dignity to beat the hell out of one of his submissive wives, to show what a fine fellow he was.

The cockerel's visit and his raucous greeting would banish sleep. The coucals would continue their dawn chorus. The leaves from the breadfruit tree that shaded the tent would fall, landing on the roof with a scrunch and then, with a secretive rustle, slide down the tent to the ground. When the leaves dried they looked like enormous brown arthritic hands, which scrunched like biscuits under my feet as I made my way down to the first cup of tea, wondering if today was the day we would be successful and get our magic-fingered Aye-aye.

The Soothsayer's Apprentices

Since Madagascar is filled with sorcerers, magicians and sooth-sayers of one sort or another, Frank thought we ought to have one in our film. Marc was duly informed that we wanted a soothsayer to tell us, for a modest fee, what our chances of catching Aye-aye were and whether we were going about it the right way. Marc said he knew of an excellent soothsayer and would contact him as soon as possible. I said we did not want any old run-of-the-mill one, but someone in the forecasting line who would be even better than Macbeth's trio of witches. Marc said that this man's credentials were impeccable and he was much in demand far and wide. So Marc sent messages to this paragon and, inevitably, we heard nothing.

The hunts went on by night and day, and Q and John began to look more and more jaded and dispirited. Time was against us. We had been searching for nearly four weeks and soon the team would have to leave and go back to Jersey. True, we had Verity, but this meant that we would not be able to include in the film all the thrills of an actual capture in the wild, and this, of course, was what they had come so far (and at considerable expense) to film. However (as I had told everyone until they were sick of hearing it), they could put Lee and me under con-tract and we would do what we were told, but they couldn't do the same to the Aye-aye. This was true, of course, but did not make the situation any happier. We were all starting to feel twitchy, not only because of the film, which was important enough, but because the capture of the Aye-aye was the whole point and purpose of the expedition in which both I and the

Trust had invested a considerable amount of money. Mealtimes were getting gloomy.

'Have you heard anything about the soothsayer?' asked Frank.

'Yes,' said Lee, 'I mean, no I haven't heard anything, but Marc knows what you want.'

'Well, jockey him along a bit,' I said. 'At least we can film the soothsayer.'

'Perhaps I should black up and do it myself?' Frank suggested.

'An excellent idea,' I said, heartily. 'How's your Malagasy coming along? We could always make it mysterious, so all you would have to do is to mumble a few words like *"Ambatondra-zaka"* or *"misaotra tompoko"*. How do you look in a loin cloth?'

Frank gave it some thought.

'Expert,' he said at length.

We were not, however, driven to those extremes, for the next morning Marc announced triumphantly that the soothsayer would be with us that very evening.

He arrived just as it got dark, a well-built man, tall for a Malagasy and with an interesting, rather imposing-looking face. Somewhat to our astonishment, he was accompanied by his mother, his wife and their four-month-old child. These, he explained, were his assistants. The baby, we asked? No, just the mother and wife. The baby was merely a spectator. It would, however, we assumed, pick up a few tips even at that age.

They all sat on the ground, smiling and talking quietly. The wife handed the baby over to its grandmother where it lay placidly, like a chocolate-coloured Michelin man. The wife shifted position and sat with her legs akimbo behind the soothsayer. He lay back and covered himself completely with a large, white *lamba*. There was a melodramatic pause, an intake of breath and then his whole body, especially his legs, vibrated violently as if he was receiving a very heavy electric shock. This meant, as had been explained to us, that he was now merely the mouthpiece of the ancestors. He took off the sheet, sat up and asked, very politely, for a beer and a cigarette. His wife explained that the soothsayer neither smoked nor drank but that the particular ancestor who was going to give us advice did both. Presumably, the means to indulge these two delicious vices were not available in the place where the ancestor was now residing but, after the first intoxicating sip had been taken and a large volume of smoke drawn luxuriously into the lungs, the ancestor was ready for business.

Naturally, the first question we asked was whether or not, in the ancestor's estimation, we would meet with any luck in our hunt. The ancestor took another draught of beer and another drag at his cigarette and said, at great length and with all the sonorousness of Sir Henry Irving in a speech from *The Bells*, that of course we were welcome if our motives were pure and not simply a cover for a colonial takeover.

At the time, this seemed to me laughable and to have more than a hint of a political speech about it. However, we were informed earnestly that country people were in constant fear that the *vazaha* would return and once more wrench their land from them. We assured the ancestor, therefore, that taking over Madagascar by force was the last thing we wanted to do and that we were merely interested in acquiring some of the country's remarkable animals to take home to show other *vazahas* what a wonderful country Madagascar was and what wonderful creatures inhabited it.

The ancestor seemed satisfied with the answer and there was silence for a bit, while he refreshed himself with more beer and luxurious puffs at his cigarette. Then he said that, our motives being pure, we would assuredly meet with success. This simple prediction took quite a long time to be delivered since, first of all, it was spoken with great verve in Malagasy and the Malagasy love long, complicated speeches with accompanying histrionics and, of course, there were appropriate pauses for refreshment.

Finally, when the beer had been consumed and the cigarette stubbed out, the ancestor went back under the *lamba* and reappeared as the soothsayer. We gave him the minuscule payment that he asked for his services and, to our astonishment, he insisted on paying us for the beer. Then, he and his entourage padded off into the night.

Whether our ultimate success was a result of intervention by the ancestor, there is no way of knowing, but certainly success attended our efforts shortly after the soothsayer's visit to us. I am in no way trying to recount this in a farcical manner, for the Malagasy take this contact with their ancestors very seriously indeed. If some people want to believe in Jesus, or Mohammed, or Buddha, or their ancestors, who is to say which is right and which wrong? It seems to me that most of the religions in the world are too dogmatic. They preach the 'live and let live' philosophy, but rarely do they practise it.

On the following evening, the local schoolmaster paid us a visit and, after a few beers, regaled us with tales of the strange, mythical fauna with which the Malagasy have peopled their landscape. You would think they had a surfeit of curious creatures in reality, without going to the trouble of inventing fictional ones. However, what the schoolmaster divulged to us were like tales from a medieval bestiary. There was one creature, for example, that looked like a gigantic cat and, apart from its fearsome aspect and its ability to kill merely by looking at you, it had an extraordinary attribute: it possessed seven livers. As it was so hostile, it was a little difficult to assess how anyone had found this out. Nevertheless, seven livers it possessed. One has heard, of course, of a cat having nine lives, but seven livers seemed excessive. I wondered to myself whether this plethora of livers was due to the fact that the animal was a heavy drinker and, if so, whether one should put it in touch with Alcoholics Anonymous.

Another magical creature is a large, rat-like beast who, should you encounter him, immediately starts to masturbate. With a serious air, you should take this curious behaviour in your stride and continue on your way. If you stop and laugh at him – and I suppose one could find a masturbating rat a subject for hilarity – he would fly into a rage and conjure up a huge storm that so alters the aspect of the forest that you become lost and may easily perish.

Another story concerns a real animal, a slender, beautiful mongoose-like creature called *Galidia*. These little animals have a penchant for chickens and, to the villagers' wrath, kill and eat them whenever they find them. The *Galidia*, it appears, is possessed of a nasty trait of character. Should it come upon a hen house that has been well constructed and is stuffed with delectable birds, the *Galidia* makes every possible attempt to get in. If the sturdiness of the structure defeats his murderous plans, he becomes frustrated and reveals the baser side of his nature. Gnashing his teeth with rage, he backs up to the hen house and proceeds to break wind through the bars. The farmer, coming out to his hen house in the morning, finds that this dastardly deed has asphyxiated all his hens, so both the *Galidia* and the farmer lose by this diabolical action. I did not ask the schoolmaster if it was possible to air condition the hen houses to obviate the risk of such a traumatic occurrence.

The abortive hunting went on apace, and the day that the television team were due to leave got nearer and nearer. We had, of course, been filming all the time and had taken a lot of footage of Verity being fed by Lee. Since the whole film was being done on tape and we had with us a mini-television set for viewing what we had filmed, we thought it might be a good idea to take it to the local school and show the children some of the shots of Verity. This would, we hoped, fulfil three functions. Firstly, we thought it would be amusing to film the children's reaction, for many of them had never seen television before. Secondly, it would show them how gentle Verity had become and how harmless. Thirdly, we hoped that the tales they would tell their parents would encourage them to help us in the Aye-aye hunting. Things did not turn out quite as we expected.

The school was a mile or so down the road and approached by a very steep, rain-gouged pathway of red laterite. It was difficult enough getting down it when it was dry and one wondered how the children managed in the rainy season when the path must have turned into something resembling one of the more difficult and dangerous ski slopes.

The school buildings were quite substantial and built of wood and brick, and our audience – about a hundred and fifty six- to ten-year-olds – sat in rows, the picture of obedience. There were only a few furtive whispers, a cough or two and the scrape of bare feet on wood as we appeared. The children regarded us with huge, dark, amazed eyes. This was the troupe of great *vazahas* who could, if aroused, eat little Malagasy children for breakfast, lunch *and* tea, so it behove them to be quiet and orderly and see what miracles we would perform.

We set up the television set so all could see and I made a short, simplistic speech saying that the Aye-aye was not a bad creature and though it ate sugar cane and coconuts, this was because the forest it used to live in had been cut down – a very bad thing for the Malagasy and the Aye-ayes – which forced them to steal the crops. Then, we started the film and, instantly, the children were riveted. There was a hiss of indrawn breath when Verity appeared and approached the front of his cage and an outbreak of astonished voices, quickly suppressed, when Lee's hand appeared holding a honey ball and they could hear her talking softly to Verity. Verity accepted the food and, when it was finished, Lee's hand appeared holding one of the fat beetle larvae. A gasp went up. So *this* is what the children had been collecting so many grubs for, to feed an Aye-aye! And they had been paid real money and given strange and delicious sweets in order to collect provender for the Aye-aye. What an extraordinary thing! Their eyes shone, their teeth gleamed as they giggled at the way Verity dealt with the grub, chewing off the head and then spooning out the contents of the still-wriggling body with his magic finger.

The film ended and the children looked as if they could have gone on watching it all day without boredom. The schoolmaster asked them to sing a song of thanks for our visit, which they did with enthusiasm. But we had another surprise up our sleeve. While they had been engrossed watching Lee feed Verity and while they sang, we had been filming them. This film we now put on.

There was a moment's stunned silence, until somebody recognized a friend. The news spread like wildfire through the ranks and, laughing and pointing, they identified their friends with wonder and – miracle of all miracles – themselves. This was better than watching boring old Aye-ayes any day of the week. To say it was a success means nothing. A combination of *The Sound of Music, Mary Poppins* and *Snow White and the Seven Dwarfs* could not have been more highly acclaimed. It was the sort of success that Hollywood moguls dream about and so rarely achieve. Naturally, it had to have a repeat performance and, then, yet another. We began to feel that it might have a longer run than *The Mousetrap* if we let it.

After this, we tried another ploy on them. We trained the camera on the class and the children could see themselves on the screen, now in close-up, now with groups of their friends. Inevitably, they waved at themselves and were convulsed with laughter when their image waved back. The children would, I think, have happily had us spend the day or even the next month with them while they revelled in our marvels. But alas, we had to leave them and return to camp, taking our sorcerer's boxes of weird tricks with us.

I had wondered why, in our hotely by Lac Alaotra, they left the television on even when there was no one in the bar, until I realized that an audience of about fifty people from the market stood on the pavement outside watching, agog, the highly-coloured and extremely explicit French soap operas through the two windows that faced the set. I believe that television has much to offer, but can have a disruptive effect. I was sure that our schoolmaster was going to have more trouble keeping his class in order after we left than he would have done trying to control a cat with seven livers.

On the way back to camp, we passed a herd of zebu, huge, placid-looking beasts with velvety skins and humps like miniature camels. This, of course, is a very common sight in Madagascar, since the beasts are revered as a symbol of social prestige. At a rich man's funeral many of his herd are killed and the graves are sometimes decorated with the horns. The novelty of the herd that we now came across was that it consisted of about ten large beasts and was under the control of and being chivvied along by a little boy with anxious eyes, who could not have been more than six and was armed with a twig as large as himself. It would be no exaggeration to say that the zebu took no notice of their shepherd. Zebu are of the definite opinion that not only roads but *everything* has been constructed for their benefit.

They meandered, they sighed, they rubbed heads, they paused to chew the cud or take a mouthful of grass from the verge. Sometimes one would turn around and slouch back the way it had come, then look astonished and offended as the little boy danced in front of it and hit it on the nose with his twig. No sooner had the boy turned it than he would discover that another one of his charges had wandered off the road and entered a small farm which, with the deep sigh of content of a gourmet greeting the first tender asparagus shoots of the year, it would proceed to plunder, until the little boy beat it back to the road, to its obvious annoyance.

The little boy danced around his herd, like a small brown moth round a large, indolent, slouching and potentially dangerous candle flame. At the sight of the Toyotas approaching, both he and the zebu displayed all the symptoms of a collective nervous breakdown. Although we stopped, the zebu milled about in an alarming way and we were afraid that one might step on the boy and crush him into oblivion without even noticing that he had gone. Fortunately, at that point, the boy's father – who had stopped for a gossip – came running and, with his stout cane, rather like a fierce sergeant-major with a parade ground full of slovenly recruits, he bashed and shouted the zebu into a more or less orderly herd and moved them past us, raising his hat and beaming at us cheerfully. The little boy looked chagrined, but as I had seen him escape what had appeared to be almost certain death two or three times, I felt he ought to be pleased at his father's interference.

It was about this time that John's dreadful ducklings made their appearance. Until then, I think they had been too young to leave their mothers, who had confined them to the village. Now they were half grown they were old enough to go foraging on their own. On the first day they appeared we could hear their excited quacking long before we saw them descending the path from the village in a single file, as excited as children going to the seaside. There were three of them: the largest was brown, as was the second largest, and the baby was white. They did everything at a smart, waddling trot, quack-quacking incessantly the while. They descended the path and disappeared over the sand-dunes in the direction of the river.

'Too small to eat roasted,' said Frank, sorrowfully. 'Might make a nice soup, though.'

John was thunderstruck.

'You couldn't *eat* them,' he protested. 'They're dear little things. I love ducks.'

'So do I, in a culinary sort of way,' said Frank.

Half an hour later, having had their swim, they appeared over the sandbank and had a conference. Obviously, our camp-site was of extreme interest to them and, after a short conver-sation as to the best means of approach, they formed a line, charged down the sandbank and waddled, quacking vocifer-ously, into our midst, tripping up Tim who was trying to carry a cup of tea to Mickey, who was feeling rotten and was con-fined to his tent. Tim almost fell flat on his face; the tea went flying.

'Bloody Hell,' he said. 'It's bad enough having cockerels shout-ing in your ear at four in the morning. Now we've got ducks all over the place.'

'Dear little things,' said John benignly. 'Sweet ickle ducky-wuckies.'

'Dear God,' said Frank. 'I'm going to sit in my tent. Tell me when Shirley Temple's finished, will you?'

Meanwhile, the ducky-wuckies were surveying our abode with wondering eyes, rather as the Malagasy children had done. What interested them most was the pile of empty, carefully-washed tins in one corner. They approached it slowly, making soft, crooning interrogative noises to each other. Then one of them leant forward and made a valiant attempt to eat a sardine tin.

'They're hungry, poor little things,' said John, and proceeded to get a stale bread roll and break it up into small pieces for them.

'You shouldn't encourage them,' I said, but it was too late. The ducky-wuckies had never come across bread in their short lives and their delight was unanimous. One of them, indeed, was so enamoured of this new delicacy that, when the bread was finished, he caught sight of a longish cigarette butt and fell on it. It stuck out of the corner of his beak, making him look like a raffish Donald Duck.

'No, no, Uncle John says no,' John intoned, picking the bird up and removing the offending stub.

'Quite right,' I said. 'They're too young to smoke.'

'Uncle John give you some more nice bready-weddy,' said John.

Of course, from that moment on, we had not a hope. The ducks would come down each morning, have a quick dip in the river and then appear over the sand-dunes, galloping down upon us like a troop of U.S. cavalry descending on a recalcitrant Indian village. They got everywhere and tried to eat everything with grim determination. We were forever tripping over or stepping on them. It is a miracle that we never killed one. They integrated themselves so closely into our daily lives that they even took siestas when and if we took them. As camp companions they were as boisterous and irritating as a litter of newly-weaned, undisciplined puppies. Then came the fatal day when the Battle of the Thunder Box took place.

While we were staying at the hotely in Mananara, we were visited by two old friends, Renée and David Winn. When living in Paris, Renée had helped look after and study the first trio of Aye-ayes and she had introduced me to the baby Aye-aye called Humphrey which inspired our expedition. When she left, Renée gave me a most useful present. It was a black plastic bag with a shower attachment. You filled this with water and laid it in the sun and within an hour or so the water was at bath temperature. Then, it could be hoisted into a convenient tree to make a hot shower unit.

We had cleared an area among the bushes which we dignified with the term 'bathroom'. In one corner was a small, palm-leaf hut in which was a large hole over which the Thunder or Bloxam Box crouched regally. From a tree hung the shower unit and beneath it a plastic sheet on which to stand. At once, we had a problem with the shower unit. If it was high enough for me to stand under, it meant that Lee could not reach the knob to turn the shower on. We puzzled over this problem for a day or two and then Lee had a brilliant idea.

'The Bloxam Box,' she said, triumphantly. 'We simply put it under the shower when you use it and you sit on it.'

I greatly looked forward to this novel experience, although I would not have been so anxious to participate in the experiment if I had known what the end result was going to be.

The next morning the Bloxam Box was duly moved, I took my seat upon it and was soon covered in soap and hair shampoo. Just at this point, the ducky-wuckies, having finished their morning swim, arrived in camp. To their astonishment, there was no one there. All the kind human beings who normally tripped over them, stamped on them, shouted at them and occasionally fed them were missing. At this moment, invigorated by soap and water, I burst into song.

The ducks were immediately galvanized into action. They came rushing round the tent, bumping into each other, falling over in their excitement and joy at having found at least one lovely human. They paused as they entered the bathroom and gazed round in astonishment. They had never been in there before, and here was one of their lovely humans sitting in a pool of water like a duck. At least, he would have been like a duck if it had not been for two things. The human was sitting on a box and the water was covered in white froth.

'Hello ducks,' I said amicably, breaking off my rendering of 'Rule Britannia'. 'Come in for a swim.'

The ducks held a rapid, muffled conference. The white stuff on the water they decided must be edible, a sort of fluffy bread, perhaps. Anyway, they decided to sample it. They waddled forward as one and dipped their beaks into my bathwater, nibbling at the froth. As they had surmised, it *was* edible, something like a sorbet smelling of lavender. They started to gobble. Alarmed at this, for I thought the froth might well contain something toxic that would harm them, I looked around for my stick, only to find that I had stupidly left it hooked over a tree branch some twenty feet away. I was unable to drive them away as they converged under the Bloxam Box.

A moment later, I was not concerned for their welfare but for my own. The Bloxam Box had a hole in the top through which (discreetly, of course) you were forced to display those parts of your anatomy not generally exposed to public view. The eldest duck looked upwards and quacked with interest. The other two looked up and quacked as well. Were these delectable morsels being displayed to them perhaps edible, a fruit new to their experience? In unison they decided to find out.

They say that my scream of pain and rage could have been heard in Antananarivo with a brisk following wind. Lee came at a run, but when she saw what was happening she just leant against a tree and had hysterics. Some wives help their husbands in an emergency, others are callous, with an approach to life that the Marquis de Sade would have applauded.

'Get these damn ducks away. Don't just stand there laughing,' I roared. 'They're trying to turn me into a bloody eunuch.'

Finally, Lee controlled herself and drove the ducks off, but from that day on I always made sure that my stick was within reach when I took a shower. I have viewed the genus *Anas* with a certain suspicion and disfavour ever since. It is a sad and humbling thought, but I don't think they would have dared to do what they did if I had been Sir Peter Scott.

I have mentioned the ducky-wuckies' attempts to eat a sardine tin. These were gathered in the camp because we washed and carefully kept every tin or box we used: in a poverty-ridden country like Madagascar, these items are of inestimable value. Bottles are treated as if they are the flasks that Shakespeare had drunk from; cardboard boxes are as reverently cared for as if they had been tea-caddies of sandalwood and amber inlaid with gold; and a sardine tin – or, better still, a corned beef tin – were worth more than any Ming vase ever created. We had decided that the distribution of this largesse should fall to our two lovely, shy maids, Veronique and Armadine, and they guarded the ever-growing pile with covetous eyes.

Veronique, we discovered, was soon to have her twentieth birthday and on one of our trips to market we searched desperately for a present for her but, alas, the town was lacking in things that gladden a maiden's heart, such as earrings or necklaces that look as if they are solid gold but would not support you in a financial crisis. At length, to our surprise, we managed to run to earth a bottle of scent, the colour and virulence of which would have immediately turned Dr Jekyll into Mr Hyde if applied, let alone drunk. Veronique was enchanted with it, but I felt somewhat guilty as I was sure that its application would reduce her matrimonial prospects by at least half, unless her suitor had lost possession of his olfactory senses.

The end of the television team's time in Madagascar was drawing near and we still had no luck. Of course, everyone was full of tales of vast hordes of Aye-aye just down the road and, when we investigated, it would turn out to be a very ancient habitation of doubtful ownership and whoever it belonged to was never at home. Now, however, our main worry was Mickey. He had – to use a north of England phrase – been feeling poorly for some time. Yet, he had conscientiously continued working and, day by day, he was beginning to look less and less like the Mick we knew and loved. We called the local doctor down and he gave Mick some injections (using our needles and syringe) but they did not bring about the rejuvenation we had hoped for. He had religiously been taking all the necessary pills and potions advised by the medical profession for those who travel in Madagascar, so his illness was a mystery. His temperature attained astronomical proportions and we were deeply worried. Mananara had (with luck) three planes a week and it was decided that Mick must be flown back to Tana, where they at least had proper nursing facilities. It is difficult to give adequate nursing attention to a large man in a tent seven feet long by three feet high. As we made the decision, the Heavens opened with glee. I think my diary entry sums up the feelings of us all:

'Heavy rain and the downpour flooded the tent. Mick worse. My hips awful because of damp, my sinuses as well. I can hardly move. Think the best thing I could do to add to the expedition is to die.'

Mick's temperature held way up in the hundreds and he became semi-delirious. It was obvious that he could not travel alone. With two of the team gone, it would put an end to any more filming, so in the end they all went. As we saw them off poor Tiana was so overcome with emotion at the thought of leaving us that he burst into floods of tears and we all had to comfort him.

The campsite seemed empty and cheerless when the team had gone. They had been wonderful people to work with and we only wished that the trip had been a greater success. Still, Roland Pas de Problème had saved our bacon by capturing Verity, otherwise the whole trip, financially speaking, would have been a total failure. We had a depressing meal that night, made all the more sombre by the candles in their bowls of sand, fluttering their way to extinction in a little graveyard of cigarette butts.

Seven egrets, who nested near the camp and had been miles away at the sea fishing, flew upstream to their roosting tree. They were breathtakingly white and quite silent as they flapped along, shining like stars against the darkening river and trees.

9

The Arrival of the Aye-aye

After lunch on the following day, Q had gone off to inspect some nests, which he gloomily predicted would turn out to be those of rats. John was shopping in town and Lee was doing something in the animal house. I wrote a bit of my diary, which had lapsed in the past couple of days, and then decided on a siesta. I chased out my friend the cockerel and his hens, who were making an insect sweep over my bed, lay down and tried to think beautiful thoughts – which was difficult, as the cockerel, annoyed by his expulsion, decided to give me a lesson in crowing. Eventually, after the third stick I had thrown had met its mark, he took the hint and wandered off up the hill.

I was just sliding off into dreams when I heard Lee calling me. I peered out of the tent from my recumbent position and saw her hurrying down the hill towards the tent, carrying in her arms what appeared to be an old sack and some chicken wire, which was in fact what it proved to be, for the chicken wire had been made into a rough cage and stuffed into the sack as a safety precaution.

'*Look* what they've brought. *Look* what they've brought,' she cried, her face lit up with joy and excitement, like a child who had been given the most splendiferous and unexpected present on Christmas Day. I looked and saw the reason for her delight.

Inside the chicken-wire cage sat an adult female Aye-aye and next to her sat her baby, one just old enough to be weaned. Obviously, the mother was scared, but the baby seemed to regard the whole experience as part of life's rich tapestry and was gazing around with huge, interested eyes and with no

137

suggestion of fear. So, twenty-four hours after the film team had left, we obtained our first Aye-aye and not one but two of these magnificent beasts.

'Come on,' I said, struggling up from my recumbent position with some difficulty. 'Let's get them into a decent cage with a nest box.'

'Isn't the baby the sweetest thing you've ever seen?' asked Lee.

'Yes, yes,' I said, 'but we can croon over it when it's properly bedded down.'

We went up the hill to the animal house, where the two beaming farmers who had caught the Aye-aye were waiting. They were delighted, of course, because not only were they ridding their farmland of a pest, but were to receive a handsome reward as well. When the cage was ready and we had, with some difficulty, persuaded the Aye-aye to leave their temporary confinement for more spacious quarters, I could see, to my intense relief, that both of them were uninjured. To my astonishment, the mother did not dive for the nest box (an important safety area for any newly-caught wild creature) but lay beside it, looking almost as if hypnotized. The baby, on the other hand, wanted to explore but never moved more than a very short way from his mother.

'Do you think she's hurt?' asked Lee, anxiously.

'No, I think she recognizes the potential danger of the situation and, because she can't know we aren't going to harm her, she's gone into a trance. The idiot baby just thinks the whole thing is an enjoyable romp but he's been taught not to move too far from mum. You can never tell how an animal is going to behave. I've had one creature feed from my hand ten minutes after capture, and another that didn't eat for three days and I thought I would have to let it go. Then it started to eat and ate me out of house and home.'

'Don't they want some food?' Lee asked.

'No, mum won't eat at this stage. She's got water and idiot child's got mum to feed off. Peace and quiet is the best.'

So we covered the cage and left them.

Down in our living-quarters we sat the two Aye-aye capturers down, gave them cigarettes and then paid them their bounty. They explained to us in great detail seven or eight times how they had captured the Aye-aye, each time with suitable embellishments and displaying a wealth of acting ability. Then they told us several times of our reaction on receiving the animals, as if we had taken no part in the scenario. It was very amusing. People have done this to me when they have read one of my books. They will recount to me at great length and with great attention to detail the entire plot and, when they are telling me about any jokes I may have made, they will recount them several times to make sure I get the point. At times, the impulse to say, 'Gosh! that book sounds fun. I must go out and buy a copy,' is almost irresistible.

When John and Q returned there was much jubilation. After all the frustration and hard work, it was as though a cloud had passed over and the sun shone again. Nobody even complained about having corned beef and sardines for the second night running. Our feelings were effervescent and, so benign did we all feel, we even allowed John to sing a verse of 'Ilkley Moor' – but *sotto voce*, for fear of upsetting our new guests.

Lee prepared their food and we went up to visit our charges. The mother had moved around a little, but she still regarded us with that expression I have seen on the faces of hospital patients when visiting hour comes round and they view with loathing the arrival of their family, carrying grapes, paperbacks, boxes of chocolates and bad news from home. The baby, however, regarded our visit as the high spot of the evening and watched with interest when Lee put in sugar cane, a coconut, honey balls, a dish of mixed fruits and another of writhing beetle grubs. He even reached out and experimented by eating a piece of banana. Meanwhile, Verity, in the next villa along the street, was making a pig of himself, but setting a good example.

The first stage had been achieved. All we had to do now, we congratulated ourselves, was to catch four more Aye-aye of the right sexes. There was nothing further we could do that night, so we went to bed and slept happily.

I awoke at dawn after a peaceful night. Our egrets, exactly on time, flapped gently down the river towards the sea and, through the mist on the river, a kingfisher flashed momentarily like an opal. The coucals were starting their liquid waterfall of calls. Then, from across the river came the 'chunk, chunk, chunk' of an axe, like the sound of nails being driven into a coffin, followed by the dying sob of a tree felled. It brought home to me how important our mission was, for each flashing axe or coup-coup blade was not only biting into the ecology of man but the shrinking kingdom of the Aye-aye as well.

We went up the hill to see what the new Aye-ayes had eaten. This is always a traumatic moment, for if the animal feeds at once you heave a sigh of relief. If it has not eaten you have to rack your brains to try to think of a way to make it eat. In this case, we hoped that the proximity of Verity eating like a pig (if I may again mix my species), would stimulate the new female's appetite. However, to our disappointment, this was not the case. Only a piece of sugar cane had been nibbled in a somewhat desultory way, and the female still regarded us with the suspicion that a spinster of long standing would greet the presence of a hippie with a guitar under her bed. Her baby took a more lenient view and was delighted that the circus had come to town once again. A certain amount of banana had been fiddled with and we suspected him rather than his mother.

It is difficult, when you have two animals in a cage, to judge the food intake of each one unless you mount a round-the-clock watch. However, in this case, we knew the baby was all right as he was still using his mother as a milk bar. All we could do was to watch the female carefully and hope that she would respond to our lavish diet soon or we would be faced with the heartbreaking task (for us) of taking them both back to where they were caught and releasing them. We said a few harsh words to Verity and told him that he was not setting a sufficiently stimulating example. There was nothing we could do but wait. The mother was in good condition and, in spite of feeding her inquisitive baby, would come to no harm if she did not eat for forty-eight hours.

That night, as we watched Verity making steady inroads on

honey balls and grubs and keeping a close eye the while on coconut and sugar cane, we thought we sensed a certain interest emanating from the abode next door, but decided that it was wishful thinking. The next morning proved us wrong. The female had eaten three grubs and parts of the honey balls. She looked much more relaxed but she still had made no attempt to enter her nest box. We had christened this new female Mina, after a Malagasy friend of ours, but we were still having arguments as to what we should call the son. That night, Mina added sugar cane to her intake, a very good sign.

Q, John and Julian had set off as usual at dusk. They were in good heart, for the arrival of Mina and her son had lifted all our spirits. They returned in triumph at about midnight, Julian beaming and giggling, Q and John trying to look as though it was every day of the week they captured an Aye-aye. She was a fine young female, glossy and beautiful. After I had examined her from every possible angle and remarked on her charms, we got her into a holding cage with little trouble.

'Was she difficult to catch?' I asked.

'No,' said Q. 'It was quite an easy tree to climb, really, compared to some. And she stayed in the nest until Julian grabbed her. It was annoying about the baby, though.'

'What baby?' I asked, startled.

'Well, she had a baby with her but during the capture the baby ran away.'

'And you left it there?' I asked.

'Well, we had to. I mean, we looked everywhere for it but I was anxious about the mother. I wanted to get her back and into a decent cage as soon as possible. Anyway, Julian says the baby will hang around the nest, so we'll go back and catch him first thing in the morning.'

'Well, I hope Julian's right,' I said. 'I don't like to think of a baby running around on its own. It may not even be weaned.'

'I'm sure we'll get it,' said John soothingly. 'Julian is convinced.'

I grunted rather sourly, for I was worried.

'Well, if he's wrong you'll have to take this female back and release it in the same spot, so that it can find its offspring.'

'Will do, will do,' said Q, placatingly.

I was very concerned about the baby, and not even the news that all our Aye-aye had fed well cured my unease. I kept visualizing the baby alone, untutored and stupid, wandering about, being pursued relentlessly by hordes of indignant Malagasy with sharp, glittering coup-coups, determined to catch the infant and hang, draw and quarter him. I imagined him coming face to face with a smooth, puma-like *Fosa* of whose existence he was ignorant and who would slap him down with a velvety paw and engulf him in one great, pink gulp. Or, horror of horrors, he might meet with the cat-like beast with seven livers, who was suffering from dyspepsia and had heard that a baby Aye-aye, taken without water, was a sure cure. Or the baby may simply be sitting, sobbing in a tree, heartbroken at the way his mother had so basely deserted him. In other words, I was working myself up into that thoroughly anthropomorphic and sentimental state which I so sternly disapprove of in others when dealing with animals.

In the morning, Q, John and Julian prepared to go out again.

'Remember,' I said, probably for the tenth time. 'You must search and search that area until you find it.'

'Yes, yes,' said Q, impatiently. 'We will.'

'And if you don't find it, you're to come straight here and get the mother and take her back there.'

'Yes, yes. I understand. I'm just as worried about the baby as you are,' said Q, aggrievedly.

I looked at him, stolid as Gibraltar. He could not possibly have my imagination, I decided.

'Well, do your best,' I said.

'I do wish you'd stop fussing,' said Lee. 'Q's just as anxious as you are about the baby. You're carrying on like a mother.'

'I am not,' I said austerely. 'I just don't like young Aye-aye of either sex wandering about the forest at night unchaperoned. You have only to peep into that intellectual newspaper, the *Sun*, to see the kind of thing that can happen.'

'Come to breakfast,' said Lee.

The early morning tea seemed to take an inordinately long time to prepare and drink. Breakfast was several centuries in reaching the table. Even a group of children bearing a plastic dish which heaved with fat, grey-white maggots did not lighten my gloom as it should have done. Then, suddenly, a shout and Q, John, Julian and his helpers came down from the road, Q bearing tenderly in his hands one of our big, white, soft collecting bags.

'We got it, we got it!' Q shouted, triumphantly. 'We got the baby – it was there just as Julian said it would be.'

I struggled up to the animal house, scarcely believing our luck. 'Uninjured?' I asked.

'Oh, yes, and easy to catch,' said John. I undid the door of the cage in which the mother resided, and Q carefully untied the bag and held the mouth of it in the doorway. I don't know what I expected, but certainly not what happened. The baby's head appeared in the mouth of the bag, huge ears turning for every sound, eyes calm and interested. He paused a moment, surveying us regally, and then stepped gracefully out of the bag and into the cage as haughtily as a princeling taking possession of his rightful kingdom. It was such a perfectly stage-managed entrance and the baby was so aristocratic and so incredibly beautiful that I stupidly burst into tears of relief.

'Thought you'd be pleased,' said Q, embarrassed on my behalf, 'not cry all over the place.'

'I *am* pleased,' I said, blowing my nose, 'and I'm not crying. It's just that Aye-aye give me hay fever, especially the baby ones.'

'Yes,' said Q. 'Very annoying.'

We watched as the baby made its way over to its mother. They both treated their reunification with no sign of emotion. You would have thought that they had never been apart. The baby, after a brief inspection of the cage, settled down to the stern business of quenching his thirst, which must have been considerable, judging by the time he took over it. We had a jubilant second breakfast and decided to call the new female Juliet after Julian who had captured her.

As usual, we nearly came to blows over what the princeling

should be christened and we only united in our condemnation when Q suggested calling it Sir Bloxam.

We now had four of our quota of six animals. We could not count Verity as he was Roland's animal, which he wanted for his island. All of them were feeding well and the babies behaved as if they had been born in captivity. Now that we had so many individuals, their behaviour was fascinating to watch, especially the incredibly dexterous use of the slender third and magic finger. As the animal moved about, this sensitive organ was constantly in use, tapping its surroundings.

As early as 1859, Sandwith meticulously described this behaviour:

> . . . bending forward his ears, and applying his nose close to the bark, he rapidly tapped the surface with the curious second [*sic*] digit, as a Woodpecker taps a tree, though with much less noise, from time to time inserting the slender finger into the worm-holes as a surgeon would a probe . . . I watched these proceedings with intense interest, and was much struck with the marvellous adaptation of the creature to its habits, shown by his acute hearing, which enables him aptly to distinguish the different tones emitted from the wood by his gentle tapping; his evidently acute sense of smell, aiding him in his search; . . . the curious slender finger, unlike that of any other animal, and which he used alternately as a pleximeter, a probe, and a scoop.

Our friend, Renée Winn, who first introduced us to Aye-aye at Vincennes in Paris, told us that she had noticed the animals tapping the coconuts they were given and thought this was to discover the level of the 'milk', so that they could determine at what point to pierce the nut. She also showed us another very curious thing. The Aye-aye were fed, among other things, a thick, rather stodgy custard in ordinary flat plastic plates. What the animals would do was to turn the plate over, chew a hole in the bottom and then extract the custard through the hole with their fingers. They did not seem able to eat the custard straight off the plate – it had be eaten through a hole for the true fulfilment of their gastronomic urges.

Just recently, the small colony at Duke University in America, which I mentioned before, has taken part in some fascinating experiments devised by Professor Erickson to try to discover how the Aye-aye finds its insect prey. Erickson's tests, to put it simply, consisted of presenting the Aye-ayes with a series of holes drilled into a log, some of which were empty, some filled with minced mealworms and others with live worms. The holes varied in design. Some were constructed in such a way that the animals were prevented from using their senses of sight and smell to detect which holes contained mealworms. The holes were also drilled at different depths beneath the surface of the log. From these experiments, Erickson concludes:

> Although visual and olfactory cues may contribute to the location and extraction of insect larvae from woody sources, these studies suggest that the aye-aye depends heavily on tapping to locate the galleries of these larvae ... The pinnae of the aye-aye are proportionately larger than in any of the other lemuroid prosimians, and it is highly likely that this species has exceptional auditory sensitivity to the movement sounds of insect larvae and to the various tones emitted in response to tapping ... The studies presented here strongly suggest that, like some bat species, this primate uses echolocation in capturing prey. None the less, tapping behaviour may serve the foraging process by providing more than auditory cues. As Sandwith indicates, the tapping behaviour is surprisingly gentle. Possibly, an exceptional cutaneous sense of the third digit provides unusual detection of and discriminability among surface vibrations. The low mass of the middle digit may allow it to resonate with the surface vibration without serious dampening. Tapping may also stimulate prey to make audible movements.

Erickson has given the Aye-aye's tapping behaviour the charming name of 'percussive foraging'.

We have so much to learn about this astonishing animal that who knows what extraordinary secrets we shall unravel in the future about the Aye-aye's magic finger. It may, indeed, prove to be more magical than even the sorcerers thought it was, and if it does prove to be echo-location or an extraordinarily developed sense of touch, it shows that once more nature is far in advance of man.

The next day, Q, John and Julian went out to look for hopeful nests and returned in an astonishingly short space of time, carrying a large male Aye-aye of pugilistic mien. Not surprisingly, he was extremely piqued at having his siesta disturbed and entered the cage with many a mighty sniff of irritation and contempt for the human race. We christened him Patrice after our second hunter, but his behaviour soon earned him the sobriquet 'the Basher'.

That evening, even before he had been fed, with great sniffs and snorts, he proceeded to examine his cage minutely and tested everything for longevity. Each wire bar on his cage was twanged for flavour, the quality of the wood of his nest box was investigated with great thoroughness and much scrunching. After he was fed, he examined his bowls minutely and hurled them about the cage to test their durability. The noise he made eating, especially his sugar cane and coconut, would have had him banished for good from Claridges or the Ritz. We decided that it was not because he necessarily wanted to escape that he was so rowdy, it was just that he was made like those humans who don't believe they are communicating properly unless they bang the table and shout. However, his boisterousness so alarmed his brethren that we had to move him to the far limits of the animal house, where his turbulent nature had a less distressing effect. I wondered if he had been born like that, or if it had come with age. So noisy was he in attracting attention to himself that I wondered why he had not attracted a well-aimed coup-coup long before now. Where silence is necessary for survival, he was attracting attention to himself with a positively suicidal raucousness.

We now had five of the six animals we were allowed to collect; we needed one more adult male, and our task was done. I simply could not believe that we had almost achieved our goal, and, moreover, within the time-limit we had set ourselves. Having got this far, it was time to have a council of war.

When we had arrived in Mananara after the bone-shattering ride from Tana, we had unanimously agreed that, if we caught any Aye-aye, it would be asking for trouble to try to transport them back to Tana over such a fiendish road. The only alternative was by air. Mananara has a tiny airstrip, with a plane to and from Tana three times a week, if you are lucky. I say 'plane' but this really is a euphemism for they all looked like relics from the First World War, and the miracle was that they were still flying and not piloted by the Red Baron.

Those of you who visit zoos and watch all sorts of exotic animals bouncing about their cages, spare a thought for the complexities that brought them there. When we left Jersey, for example, we had absolutely no idea whether we would obtain the creatures we wanted or return empty-handed. On the off-chance that we *would* get Aye-aye, cages in our quarantine area had to be refurbished to take an animal who, it appeared, was quite capable of chewing its way out of Sing Sing. This *had* to be done, for if we were successful in getting Aye-aye we wanted them back in Jersey as soon as possible, not waiting around until cages were ready for them.

The first thing, though, was to get the animals we had out of Mananara to Tana and to alert Jersey that we had been success-ful. Our travelling cages for our charges would not fit into the ordinary Red Baron-type aeroplane, and we didn't want to rely on the haphazard schedules of commercial flights. So, we decided that the best thing to do was for Lee and me to fly to Tana, alert Jersey, and hire a plane.

The time came for us to leave. Both Lee and I were sorry; I particularly so, for I had grown very fond of the camp, which was very beautiful, and the only thing that marred it for me was my immobility. We would both miss the daily life there: the scandalized or hysterical reception of the ferryman's verbal newspaper delivery; the bucket girl and her songs; the other sedate ladies with their washing, who moved closer and closer to the team as they bathed naked, presumably to reassure them-selves that their menfolk were just as anatomically good as any

147

vazaha; the coucals' liquid calls, sliding in the day; the solemn-faced children bringing in grubs for our precious animals and being paid in small coin or sweets. We would remember the little boy who, together with his four-year-old sister, brought in a grub, carefully wrapped in a leaf, a grub almost microscopically tiny. We gave him a large, malevolently-coloured sweet, and watched him as he carefully bit it and gave half to his sister; the little group of children who, on being given half a bottle of lemonade, carefully passed it from one to another, each taking a sip, not a gulp, until the bottle was empty. All these had become part of our lives, and even the cockerel and his hens and the thrice-cursed ducky-wuckies had become our friends and illuminated our lives, however briefly.

Our faithful Marc wept, as did our two sweet, gentle ladies. Their grief was not assuaged by the ever-growing pile of tins, bottles and boxes which it would be their happy task, ultimately, to distribute among their nearest and dearest. We drove through the village, exchanging waves, filling our lungs for the last time with the rich mélange of exotic scents, the musk of cloves, the sweetness of vanilla, the welcoming smell of cooking fires and that subtle, indefinable smell of sunlight on green leaves. Under a lychee tree blushing with fruit, three zebu lay taking the shade, as Captain Bob used to put it, and against the silky warm flank of one of them their six-year-old herder lay asleep, his twig, his Excalibur, lying in his limp hand.

We got to town and made our way to the hotely to have a drink and say farewell to Madame. There was the steady 'trink, trink, trink' of the crystal hammers and, as we left for the airport, I scooped up a small handful. Earlier that morning, like a love-sick Victorian maiden (which I in no way resemble), I had plucked some of the curiously shaped leaves from the plants that grew around our tent and pressed them in my somewhat haphazard diary. The fact that they all fell out and were lost on the way back to Jersey is neither here nor there.

We arrived at the grass airstrip just as the plane landed. We boarded and I got the immediate impression that our transport seemed to have been designed – in a moment of mental aberration – by Snow White for her dwarfs. We sat in minute seats that were so close together that our knees were rammed tightly against the back of the seat in front, a uncomfortable position, to say the least. The plane was built to carry sixteen passengers and to say that we closely resembled a well-packed sardine can is no exaggeration.

I whiled away the time before take-off by reading a flight pamphlet with the fascinating title *Fepetra Rahatra Doza* (For Your Safety). It had a picture of the plane, showing all the emergency exits, none of which, it seemed to me, we could get to, compressed together as we were. Next came a riveting picture of what you should do in an emergency, which was to lean forward and place your head between your knees. This also seemed to me to be an impossibility, even if one was a professional contortionist.

Worse was to follow. The pamphlet informed me that there was a life jacket under every seat. I made a careful inspection of all the seats I could see, including my own, and there were no life jackets. On further inspection, I found the life jacket on the back of the seat in front encased in a plastic packet that would require a pickaxe to make the jacket emerge. The slim, jolly and romantic lady in the pamphlet appeared, from the illustration, not only to have extracted it but to have put it on in record time, so as to do an elegant swallow dive into the Indian Ocean when the plane hit the sea.

I examined the whole scenario with care and came to the reluctant conclusion that it was not sound. In an emergency, we would all dutifully try to wedge our heads between our knees, which would then be held firmly in place by the back of the seat in front. The dimensions of your skull would be crucial to this procedure and from the cries of pain you would easily be able to detect the passengers with the greater brain capacity (the more Neanderthal ones achieving success with mere groans of anguish).

Having got your head into the correct position, supposing you were informed by the pilot that you were going to hit the sea and not the land? Immediate panic would undoubtedly ensue. You would have to wrench yourself up from your foetus-like position and put on your life jacket. The less observant passengers would, of course, not be able to find theirs under their seats, thus increasing a certain sense of doom and despondency. Supposing, then, that they ascertained the true position of their life jackets and borrowed each other's Swiss army knives to dissect the plastic to get them out – there would not be room for us all to put them on simultaneously. We would have to do it one at a time, the women and children first, naturally.

By the time we had achieved this, I feared, the plane would be full fathom five among the sharks before you could say *Fepetra Rahatra Doza*. I closed my eyes and tried not to think of mechanical faults as the plane took off, uncertain as a butterfly.

The Flight of the Magic Finger

We returned to Tana without mishap and, as a compensation for the quantity of sardines and corned beef we had been forced to consume, we treated ourselves to a magnificent dinner at the Hotel Colbert, starting with two dozen oysters each and ending via a cream meringue with a very good local cheese. Full as pythons that had eaten an entire pygmy village, we went to our bedroom and Lee started on the tortuous round of telephone calls and faxes that were necessary to get our act together. When you see an animal in a zoo, spare a thought for the person who got it there. The burden of this fell on Lee since she spoke such good French, whereas my command of that language has been described by my French friends as closely approaching something spoken by a Spanish cow, the most insulting thing one can say about an Englishman speaking what he fondly believes is *français*.

Let me enumerate the things that had to be done. Firstly, a long fax had to be sent to our Zoological Director, Jeremy Mallinson, boasting of our success and giving minute details of each Aye-aye's likes and dislikes, together with the likes and dislikes of the entire collection, from Gentle lemurs to Jumping rats. Secondly, what appeared to be ten thousand telephone calls had to be made to find out if there was a small freight plane we could hire. Naturally, we did not want to spend money on something the size of Concorde, even supposing that such a plane could land on an airfield which was about as big as a child's handkerchief.

To our surprise, we ran a plane to earth without too much

trouble. Mathematics now entered our discussions: we had to negotiate the price in Malagasy francs while remembering simultaneously how many pounds sterling we had left and had to provide the weights and dimensions of the travelling cages (which we had carefully written down in pounds and inches) to the Malagasy in metric figures. I have considered myself to be an unrecognized mathematical genius ever since, at the age of eight, I managed to add five and four together and get the rather surprising total of twenty-eight. Brushing aside my protestations that I was, in reality, an unsung Einstein, Lee told me to go out and enjoy myself in the *zoma* while she, with her more agile, slippery eel-like feminine mind, dealt with these problems.

Our troubles now centred on the scheduling of the plane. As it was the height of the lychee season and people were flying lychees in all directions, this was difficult. But it was vital that the plane carrying Q and our valuable creatures should arrive in Tana to coincide with the international flight. In addition to this somewhat complex arrangement, we had to find a driver, for even John, with his manifold talents, could not ferry *two* Toyotas back to Tana over those unspeakable roads. Once more, the dreaded lychees (a fruit I loved but learned to hate) entered our lives. All the best drivers were busy rushing to and fro with lorry-loads of the delectable and delicate fruit. Finally, however, we managed to track down one driver who had the time to undertake our mission.

Now another problem reared its ugly head. We had to let John and Q know of our success in hiring a plane and the exact timing of its arrival in Mananara so that the Aye-aye (until now occupying spacious holding cages) would be ready to go in their travelling crates for the flight to Tana. To accomplish this would take some time, so the sooner John and Q knew the better. There were three ways of getting the news to them: through the local postal service, the radio in Roland's office, or someone flying up to Mananara, to whom we could entrust a cleft stick. As all telephonic communications had been installed by the benevolent Mao Tse-tung, they worked about as well as the locks on hotely bedrooms. We took no risks, and sent messages by all the routes.

That evening, I attempted to revive my exhausted wife (who had been on the telephone since eight o'clock in the morning) by giving her another sumptuous oyster feast. She found what she thought was a pearl in one of them and thought it was a good omen, until she disgorged it and we found that it was a battered and furtive-looking clove. When I attracted the waiter's attention to this rather surprising symbiosis he nodded, gave me a splendid, congratulatory smile, said 'Oui, monsieur', filled my glass and departed. Apparently in his philosophy you did not question good luck.

In the midst of all this, it was an unexpected and unpleasant blow to learn of my elder brother's death. He had always been my mentor and, indeed, it was he who encouraged me to take up writing. At that range there was nothing very positive I could do to comfort his widow, his numerous ex-wives and his one surviving daughter, except to send them news of our probable date of arrival in Jersey. However, this bit of gloomy news was tempered slightly by the information that Mickey, after a terrible time in Tana with what was finally diagnosed as cerebral malaria, had finally flown back to Jersey and was well on the road to recovery.

Apparently, when the team had got Mickey back to Tana, he was delirious and had to be given a blood transfusion and kept on a drip for a time. The Malagasy nurses found that he was too strong for them and he kept tearing his drip out. So Captain Bob and Tim had to take over the nursing, holding him down when he got obstreperous and preventing him from pulling out all the life-saving equipment with which he was festooned. It was wonderful to hear that our amiable and lovable friend was going to get better. Apart from anything else, it gave us the excuse to open a bottle of champagne to drink to both my brother – a gesture he would have appreciated – and to Mick's recovery.

The pace now hotted up. Having found the plane and the driver, Lee had to dive into the murky depths of bureaucracy because our all-important export permits had to be obtained from the correct Ministry. The gentleman who was supposed to issue these always seemed to be out. When tracked to his lair, we observed a thick coating of dust on his telephone, which seemed to prove that he had solved this irritant of office by simply not answering it. (Of course, it may have been simply there to impress. I know that in Argentina and Paraguay no official can be treated as an official until he has reposing on his desk one of those jolly little merry-go-rounds from which hang at least twenty-five impressive stamps. This he never uses, but twists in a meditative way while thinking out new ways of obstruction.)

Having got our export permits, next we had to get our vitally important C.I.T.E.S. permit signed. Albeit filled with many loopholes, C.I.T.E.S. (the Convention on Trade in Endangered Species) is a splendid step towards stopping illegal trafficking in rare wild animals, plants and their products. The wildlife trade can be counted in billions of dollars a year; and wildlife means everything from orchids to elephants. Much of this trade is illegal because the animals and plants concerned are threatened with extinction. Those animal lovers who complain about zoos and try to put a stop to the important work in breeding rare species which they undertake, should turn their attention to the real issues. Between 1980 and 1981, over 33,000 wild-caught parrots passed through Amsterdam airport. Most of these either die on their journey or shortly afterwards because to save costs they are squashed together as slaves used to be. If they survive, they are sold to 'bird lovers' in different parts of the world.

Japan and Hong Kong are steadily whittling away at the last of the elephants, turning their tusks (so much more elegant left on the elephant) into artistic carvings. In much the same way, the beautiful furs from leopard, jaguar, Snow leopard, Clouded leopard and so on, are used to clad the inelegant bodies of thoughtless and, for the most part, ugly women. I wonder how many would buy these furs if they knew that on their bodies they wore the skin of an animal that, when captured, was killed by the medieval and agonizing method of having a red-hot rod inserted up its rectum so as not to mark the skin.

In a desperate attempt to preserve anything from cacti to crocodiles, 113 countries have signed C.I.T.E.S. so far. At the moment, however, signing the Convention is merely a gesture of intent and carries no legal weight if the country chooses to ignore it. Even so, C.I.T.E.S. is a positive start. A bigger stumbling block to the effectiveness of the Convention is the fact that the poor Customs officers are not biologists and so cannot be expected to distinguish between a frog with yellow spots on a green background (in which trade is legal), and one with yellow spots on a purple background (in which trade is illegal). In spite of their somewhat shaky zoological and botanical knowledge the Customs officers have pulled off some notable coups (including one that involved about seventy Radiated tortoises that ended up in our reptile house until we could find homes for them). It is to be hoped that C.I.T.E.S., for all its faults, is the start of the control and eventual elimination of this cruel and disastrous trade in living organisms.

At last, the preliminary bureaucratic bookwork was done and we could only look forward to Q's arrival in Tana with our Aye-ayes. As we waited at the airstrip, we visualized everything that could have gone wrong: John and Q had not received our message and were only now, at this very moment, trying to get indignant Aye-ayes into their travelling boxes; the plane had never arrived, or, if it had, was now heading back to us empty or, worse still, full of our lovely beasts, but crashing to its doom somewhere in central Madagascar. Even if all these dire prognostications were proved untrue, would the plane arrive in time to match up with the other's departure? We had been shocked early that morning to be informed that the cargo-hold on Air Madagascar was not pressurized and the temperature would drop to 4°C. Panic-stricken, we rushed out to the *zoma* and bought dozens of cheap blankets to wrap the cages in, only to find out at the airport that our information was incorrect and we were the proud owners of the biggest stock of unnecessary blankets in Tana.

Not unnaturally, our nerves were in something of a flutter as we watched our hire plane land and taxi towards us. When Q emerged, wearing his usual inscrutable expression, we were quite prepared to be told that all the Aye-aye had escaped during the night. Instead of which, he informed us of the splendid news

155

that after Lee and I had left two more Aye-aye, a female and a male, had been captured. This meant that we had not only provided our saviour, Roland, with a mate for Verity, but had caught the full complement of the animals allowed us by the Government. There was no time for backslapping and congratulatory drinks, however, for we had to get the animals over to the Customs export shed.

Things now became even more complex and we had some heartstopping moments. We discovered, with horror, that Q had lost all his money *and* his traveller's cheques. This was serious, for the Malagasy authorities take careful note of how much cash you bring into the country and check it again when you leave, to make sure you have not been using your pounds illegally to buy Malagasy francs at a reduced rate on the black market. By the Grace of God, our old friend Benjamin Andriamahaja was in Tana and not on holiday. A frantic phone call to the Ministry of Higher Education had him up at the airport in a trice. In our estimation, Benjamin is *the* Mr Fixit in Madagascar. Within an hour or so, Q's name was cleared and he did not have to go to prison for life.

Naturally, though all of our collection was immensely valuable, the Aye-aye headed the list and we felt it was important that they should get to Jersey as quickly as possible. Tsimbazaza Zoo, where we had housed the rest of our collection, had no proper accommodation for Aye-aye, so the plan was for Q to accompany them to Mauritius, feed them, keep them overnight and put them on the London flight the next day. In London, they would be met by Jeremy and staff and Q, having acted as nursemaid as far as Mauritius, was to return to Madagascar and join us to help pack up the rest of the animals. To do this, he needed a re-entry visa. Inspection of his much-battered passport revealed the fact that he had no page on which the re-entry visa could be stamped. Immediately, panic ensued and Q and Benjamin took a frantic taxi ride to the British Embassy in search of another page. The Embassy, which up until now had been courteous and helpful, dealt us a body blow. They could not issue pages, only whole passports, and they didn't have any. So we had to hope that Q could get a new passport from the High Commission in Mauritius and then get the re-entry visa from the Malagasy Consulate there.

In the event, things worked out smoothly, but when you are ferrying such a precious cargo of wild creatures from one side of the world to the other, every hiccough in the bureaucratic system shortens your life expectancy.

That evening, Q phoned to tell us that the first stage of the journey had gone off without a hitch. The Aye-aye had been bedded down and fed and he was going to be allowed to stow them personally in the cargo hold of the plane for London. The next day, we received a fax from Jeremy to reassure us that he had chartered a plane to carry the animals from London to Jersey, where a huge supply of all the delicious foods we had asked him to acquire was awaiting them. Later, Q phoned to say that he had successfully loaded the animals on to the London flight, and they all looked very perky. All we could do now was pray.

The next day, the British Ambassador, Dennis Amy, once again came to our rescue. So many friends of our friends had helped us that it was impossible to entertain them individually to thank them. What we needed was a party.

'Good idea,' said Dennis, 'bring 'em all to my little place for a knees-up.'

And a sumptuous knees-up it was. Nearly everyone we had met was there: dear Madame Berthe from Benjamin's ministry, whom we had known for more than ten years; Benjamin himself; Messrs. Raymond and Georges and Mme Celestine from the *Eaux et Forêts* Ministry, who had given permission and encouragement for the expedition in the first place; Barthélémi and his lovely wife, Colette; Martin, Lucienne and Olivier from the World Wide Fund for Nature; Mihanta with his evermore grin. It was a splendid party and what put the gilt on the gingerbread was the fact that reposing in my pocket was a fax from Jeremy which read:

'Delighted to record that all six Aye-aye arrived *safely* at JWPT and are in their respective quarters. Mina and juvenile were taking banana and eating sugar cane on flight over from London, whereas Alain was studying the world from the security of his nest box, Juliet was curled up with infant and Patrice was curled up in similar fashion. Mina and juvenile already out of their box in spacious 'bat quarantine' area and eating already.

'We all could not be more impressed and delighted with the success of the Durrell Expedition. Congratulations to all concerned.'

It was a wrench to leave Madagascar – a place so full of extraordinary life forms, an island we loved dearly and one we hoped that we might help even more in the future. Lee and Q undertook the task of crating up our Gentle lemurs and other animals for the journey and no mishaps occurred. (An escaped animal at the last minute can make your hair turn grey.) While they were doing this, John and I ferried our equipment to the airport for the flight to Mauritius.

As the day was overcast and drizzly, I slipped on a lightweight French fishing jacket which I'd worn throughout our expedition and, as we were waiting for our flight to be called, I discovered two pieces of paper in my pocket. One was the form which you had to fill in to stay in the hotely in Morandava. This bureaucratic absurdity takes place all over the world, of course, and somewhere there must be a gigantic building (designed by Kafka, perhaps) in which all these useless bits of paper gently simmer and moulder away as an example of mankind's folly to mankind. I had kept this one, however, because one of the questions it asked intrigued me. The form read like this:

(1) *Preciser bien s'il agit de Mr, Mme ou Mlle*
(Precise of Mr, Mrs or Miss)
(2) *Passeport, C.N.I., I.E, Permis de conduire*
(Passport. Licence driver)
(3) *Rayer les mentions inutiles*
(Keeps of the useless means)

I fear I shall go to my grave baffled and uncertain as to whether or not I am a keeps of the useless means.

The other piece of paper showed what purported to be a crashed plane with a chute out of the door, down which a smiling lady was shown sliding with all the *sangfroid* of someone to whom this happens with monotonous regularity. Underneath the French caption was written the mysterious translation:

'Sit one the thrush and skid feet first.'

I remembered I had kept it to show the Royal Society for the Protection of Birds and ask them what they intended to do about it. These two bits of paper made a fitting souvenir as we boarded the plane and flew away from Madagascar towards Mauritius.

Lee and I decided that we would stay on for a few days in Mauritius, inspecting one of our major conservation projects, now in its fifteenth successful year. Carl Jones, our man in Mauritius, was there to meet us with his gangling limbs, brown hair like some sort of uncontrollable seaweed, sparkling eyes, a wide, warm grin like one of the more lovable ventriloquists' dummies and a voice that tried itself out from deep bass to the faint squeak made by a newly-born bat.

'So you've come to see a proper set-up at last, have you?' he said. 'Left all those mangy lemurs and come to see some decent birds. Be a real education for you to see some birds after all those lemurs . . . Ugh! . . . Saw those Aye-ayes, horrible things, they were. What d'you want them for when you can have a real Mauritian kestrel? Daft you are.'

'If you go on besmirching lemurs in this way,' said Lee, firmly, 'I shall borrow Gerry's stick and make you into a permanent falsetto, not a part-time one.'

Carl spends a lot of his waking moments practising to be an eccentric. He is doing splendidly at it but has a long way to go before he reaches the heights of some of his zoological predecessors. Buckland, for example, made a pie out of a deceased rhinoceros at London Zoo and transported it with him to hand out on a lecture tour to the 'working classes' in the north of England. Waterton had a nasty and painful infestation of 'jiggers' in his feet while in Guyana, but left them *in situ* so that, on the long, slow voyage back to England, he could observe at what point the decreasing temperature killed them. True, when you

159

open Carl's fridge to get a beer, you can never be quite sure whether a baby dolphin or a concourse of dead mongoose is liable to fall out. But this is a long way from Buckland, who hauled a dead Bengal tiger up the front of his house in London by ropes and pulleys to get it into the attic where he could dissect it.

Our fifteen-year association with the Mascarene Islands dates back to the time when I chose Mauritius for a holiday. After all, we had picked the fantastic Dodo as our symbol, since it was a bird discovered on Mauritius in 1599 and had vanished by 1693, thus summing up what man is doing to the world in general. However, on reaching the island, I found there were other things in peril of following the Dodo to extinction. The Mauritian kestrel, for example, was endangered by the felling of its forest home and wholesale spraying with insecticides. There were only four known birds left in the world. The beautiful Pink pigeon's numbers had dwindled until there were just twenty birds. On nearby Rodrigues, the beautiful golden fruit bat which is native to the island now numbered only 120. On Round Island, a small islet off Mauritius, unique reptile and plant populations were threatened by the ecological havoc wrought by rabbits and goats foolishly introduced there in the early nineteenth century.

It was clear that the Mascarene flora and fauna desperately needed a helping hand. The International Council for Bird Preservation had attempted to start a captive breeding unit for the kestrel and the pigeon which, unfortunately, had been unsuccessful and no one was doing anything about the Rodrigues fruit bat or the strange reptiles of Round Island. My holiday became work.

With the agreement and help of the Mauritian Government, we caught a small colony of bats and three groups of Round Island reptiles to take to Jersey to found breeding colonies. Meanwhile, we and the Government made the most strenuous efforts to rid the island of its malignant plague of rabbits and goats. We finally succeeded with the help of the New Zealand Wildlife Service, well versed in ways of ridding islands of unpleasant intruders, and (believe it or not) the Australian Navy, who lent us a helicopter to ferry our team and equipment to the island. Meanwhile, we agreed with the I.C.B.P. to take over the problem of the pigeon and the kestrel, in spite of the fact that there seemed little hope of saving either species.

In conservation, the motto should always be 'never say die'. A small group of pigeons was caught up: half were left at the Government breeding station at Black River in Mauritius and the rest sent to Jersey. We had an uphill struggle with the pigeons but, finally, we learnt the trick of supplying what they wanted and, gradually, had success. Today, through captive breeding efforts in both Mauritius and Jersey, the pigeon population has risen from the original twenty wild birds that we found to one hundred and fifty in captivity. Although the major breeding colonies are in Mauritius and Jersey, as a further safeguard we have founded small colonies in zoos in England and America. Our job is not yet complete, of course, for the original gene pool is small and this may cause problems in the future. But at least we can say that we have built up the numbers of birds so we have specimens with which to experiment. Trying to save a bird whose numbers had dropped to twenty individuals is a very precarious conservation tightrope walk.

The kestrels' situation was even worse, because only four birds were known to be left. Carl waited his chance and as soon as one pair nested he collected the eggs and took them to the aviaries at Black River. (If you take eggs in this way, it is almost certain that the parents will lay again, so the action is not quite as irresponsible as it sounds.) At Black River, European kestrels had been held in readiness to act as foster parents when the precious eggs hatched and Carl was also prepared for handrearing, should that prove necessary. This was the beginning of Carl's brilliant work with the kestrel, aided greatly by the Peregrine Fund in the U.S.A. If ever anyone can be said to have snatched a species back from the brink of oblivion, then it can be said of Carl and this diminutive hawk. Using old falconers' techniques, Carl had returned 112 young kestrels to the wild by 1990 – a prodigious feat.

When we arrived in Mauritius from Madagascar, we had successful breeding colonies of Pink pigeon, kestrel and Rodrigues fruit bat in both Jersey and Mauritius. We had Round Island geckos, skinks and boas overflowing from our cages in the Reptile House in Jersey and the problem of introduced pests to Round Island had been solved. It was time for me to update myself on the Mauritian side of the operation.

Carl drove us up to the Macchabe/Brise Fer forest, which was the new release site for captive-bred pigeons, some of them from our aviaries in Jersey. Mauritius is a fascinating island, with strange, twisted mountains that look like the backdrop of a film set by Dali. Everywhere you look there are a thousand different greens, lush and tropical. Look more closely, however, and you will see that ninety per cent of the vegetation has intruded from another part of the world and is slowly edging the indigenous plants to extinction. The view delights the untutored eye of the tourists, for out of this brilliant panoply of plants, saucer-sized hibiscus flowers, large and red as setting suns, bougainvillaea like pink and salmon cloaks of flowers thrown haphazardly, they expect Tarzan and Jane, fingers entwined, to emerge with a retinue of faithful chimpanzees. Fortunately, Mauritius has not, thus far, become quite as degraded as that.

The Macchabe forest is one of the last pieces of indigenous forest left in Mauritius and it was chosen as a release site for the pigeons because here they have plenty of space and a natural food supply. We came to a small camp, a neat cluster of tents where the pigeon guardians and watchers lived. Each bird could be identified by the coloured ring on its ankle and some are radio-equipped so that they could be more easily tracked in the thick forest. The pigeons, of course, come under the closest scrutiny, so we would know who was mating with whom, who was eating what, and whereabouts in the forest all this was taking place.

In spite of being led by a dedicated madman like Carl and having to live in fairly primitive conditions, the team looked happy and seemed to be enjoying its work. It has always amazed me that these people who are trying to learn and understand the world around us before it is bulldozed out of existence, have to work on piteously low salaries or on minuscule and precarious grants, while they do one of the most important jobs in the world. For it is only by learning how the planet works that we will see what we are doing wrong and have a chance to save it and ourselves as well.

As we were sitting around chatting and receiving firsthand news of the project, something delectable happened. There was a sudden rustle of wings and a Pink pigeon flew into the tree twenty feet above us. Moreover, to our astonishment it was one of the birds we had bred in Jersey and sent out as part of the re-introduction scheme, as we could tell by its ring. It preened briefly and then sat there, full bosomed, beautiful, wearing the vacuous expression all Pink pigeons have, looking exactly like one of the more unfortunate examples of Victorian taxidermy. Of course, we gave it news of its brethren, which it received in a stoical manner and presently it flew off into the forest.

When I accused Carl of having stage-managed the whole thing, he swore on the grave of that noted pigeon fancier, Lloyd George, that this was not so. It was heart-warming to see a Jersey-bred bird perching on a tree in its island home: that is what zoos – good zoos – are all about.

The next day, we set off in the Government helicopter to Round Island, flying low over the brilliant-green sugar-cane fields, each decorated with mounds of volcanic rock too big to be shifted and looking like gargantuan elephant droppings. As we left Mauritius and flew out over the sparkling blue water, we could see Round Island lying ahead of us like the top half of a mis-shapen tortoise shell. It was 1986 before we were sure that we had solved the rabbit problem on the island and the last of these pests had been eliminated. Now the two rare species of palm, which had been planted in safety in the Pamplemousses Botanical Gardens, could be returned to their rightful home and the plant life left on the island could seed and grow in peace, free from the gastronomical attentions of both rabbits and goats.

We landed, in a great cloud of dust, on what is called – euphemistically – the helipad and is, in fact, the only flat bit of the island a helicopter *can* land on. To the untutored eye, the island still looked like a huge piece of terracotta and grey clay that had been whirled around by a gigantic egg whisk and poured out onto the surface of the sea, a terrain that was, in miniature, like a Doré drawing of a piece of Dante's Inferno. To the discerning eye, patches of green were appearing on the valley edges and in flat places, to us as gay as banners. Under the fan palms which had seeded were growing little regiments of their offspring, holding up their small green blades like a vegetable Pretorian guard, ready to march and colonize the bleak, hot continent of tuff. This new growth had produced a wonderful chain reaction, for the insect life had proliferated which, in turn, meant that the geckos and lizards had more to eat and were becoming fatter and more glossy, and that they, in their turn, were providing more food for the rare boa. What we had succeeded in doing was reversing the process brought about by man's stupidity.

The island, once thickly forested by palms and hardwoods, such as ebony, had been deforested by the introduction of two of the beasts most detrimental to green growth. They had eaten the island almost bald and the wind and the rain were eroding what tuff remained and drowning it in the sea. Now, with our help, it had a chance of recovery. Now we could bring back its tiny palm savannah and, hopefully, plant hardwoods that would spread over its miniature mountain range. It will take years and years of careful guardianship yet to return the island to its original state, but all the component parts are there and working. So we can truly say that, with the assistance of the Mauritian Government and many other people from all over the world, our Trust in Jersey has saved unique Round Island, the island that almost died. It is something we are very proud of and, although in fifty years we who have taken part in this will not be around, I hope that countless other people will take delight in our achievement.

Carl had promised me that, on the evening before we left, I could see captive-bred kestrels that had been returned to the wild. We drove out to one of the many areas where he has reintroduced this diminutive hawk. It was a large, flat area, part sugar-cane field, partly the remaining stubble of a maize crop. The backdrop was a beautiful series of forested hills, undulating across the horizon like green waves. The sky was a soft blue with fragments of pink cloud dabbed here and there across it.

'Now,' said Carl, handing me a rather forlorn-looking dead mouse that he produced from his pocket. 'Just go and stand over there and hold the mouse aloft while I call them.'

I stood in the stubble and held up the mouse obediently, feeling like a macabre and portly Statue of Liberty. Now Carl started a series of 'cooee' noises, the soprano part of his voice coming into its own. This went on for some time and my arm started to ache.

'Here they come!' Carl shouted suddenly.

There was the faintest angel's breath of disturbed air, a flash – like an eye-flick – of a brown body, a gleaming eye, the gentlest touch of talons on my fingers as the mouse was deftly removed and the hawk flew off with it. It was an astonishing experience to have this bird, of which there had been only four specimens in the wild and which was now, with the aid of captive breeding, well on the road to recovery, swoop down from the sky like a dart and take a mouse from my fingers. Carl's broad grin and shining eyes showed that he appreciated his hard work and success as much as I did.

The next day we left for London, but as we lumbered along in the huge plane I could still feel the gentle scrape of the kestrel's talons on my knuckles like a caress.

When we arrived in Jersey it was freezing cold and, through some oversight, we were clad in our tropical clothing. We shivered our way off the plane and into the Manor House, where we managed to get our blood temperature above zero by the application of malt whisky and every warm garment we possessed. Then came the glorious moment we had been waiting for – to see the lovely creatures we had gathered from Madagascar.

We admired the beautiful Kapidolo, their shells a-gleam, their wonderful cream moustaches looking as though they had just emerged from the loving hands of an expert barber. Then our beautiful snakes, smooth and warm as sea-sanded pebbles, one as plump as a favourite *houri*, which led us to suppose that she had been having a successful affair with another boa before she fell into our hands. We reminisced with Q about how, when we were discussing the campsite (a million years ago) one of these svelte snakes had slid across it, thus assuring our unsuperstitious minds of success. Then, since the combination of our clothing and the temperature in the Reptile House was rapidly liquefying us, we went to visit the Jumping rats.

These extraordinary creatures had settled in with such aplomb that you would have thought it had been agreed unanimously at a recent neighbourhood meeting that all Giant Jumping rats should emigrate to Jersey where job and jumping opportunities, housing, food prices and so on were all superior to Morandava and (they had heard) there were fewer flies. They had settled down beautifully and – so far – had given us none of the heart-stopping problems that some newly-caught animals can give. I began to have a suspicion that these creatures possessed greater intelligence than some of the lemurs and it behove us to keep an interested eye on them.

Next, we went to see our lovely lake-dwellers, the Gentle lemurs, now at last housed in spacious cages in our quarantine section. All of them looked good. Their fur – which is a useful barometer of their well-being – had fluffed out. Edward had grown considerably and was now displaying the beginnings of a belligerent mien. Araminta looked in good form with cumulous fur and an air of superiority just like her namesake.

Finally, we came to the fabulous creatures we had gone so far to collect and to protect, our little tribe of magic-fingered ones. The first one I had ever met had given me a shock, an extraordinary fibrillation of the nerves, a sense of astonishment that no other animal has given me. And yet I have met everything from Killer whales to hummingbirds the size of a flake of ash, animals as curious as giraffe to platypus. Now to see Aye-aye, at last, in Jersey, exploring their cages with eyes that, unlike other lemurs, are focussed and seem to have a keen brain behind them, to learn that they had settled down and were feeding well was a tremendous relief. One felt one was on the edge of some enormous undertaking.

Bryan Carroll, our Curator of Mammals, opened a cage and an Aye-aye came running to him. He lifted it out and handed it to me. It was the little princeling Q had caught – huge ears, magnificent, calm, but interested eyes of the loveliest colour, his strange hands, black and soft and his magic finger crooked like a Victorian button hook. I thought of the animals we had just seen in Mauritius and what we had achieved for them. If only we could do the same for this strange cargo of creatures we had returned with. If, with our help and the help of others, remnants of the wonderful island of Madagascar can be saved and we can return the princeling's progeny to them that, in some way, would be man's apology for the way he has treated nature.

The princeling looked at me with shining eyes, his ears moving to and fro. He sniffed my beard and combed it gently. Then, with infinite care, he inserted his magic finger into my ear.

We had come full circle but, as we all know, circles have no end.

Epilogue

I hope that, having read this book, you will want to know more about the future of our lovely Aye-aye, Gentle lemur, Giant Jumping rat and Ploughshare tortoise. Indeed, I hope this book has made you more conscious of, and concerned for, the many small, obscure species which face obliteration unless something is done to rescue them.

I get letters from people all over the world, telling me how concerned they are about our gross mis-management of the planet and my advice to them has always been: join your local conservation society so that you can have a voice; worry your M.P., Congressman, or whoever represents you, into a nervous decline by consistently telling them where you think they are going wrong; and join us.

We will send you full details of all our multi-faceted activities, including details of our unique fund-raising scheme called S.A.F.E. (Save Animals From Extinction).

We are not only building up breeding colonies of rare species here on the island of Jersey, we are doing it overseas as well. We are training people from many different parts of the world in the art of captive breeding to aid conservation and we are releasing captive-bred animals to the wild when the time is right. We consider this work to be of vital importance and we should be delighted if you would join us. You may write to me here at:

> Jersey Wildlife Preservation Trust,
> Les Augrès Manor,
> Trinity,
> Jersey JE3 5BF.

Or, if you live in the U.S.A., write to our sister organization, Wildlife Preservation Trust International, at:

3400 W. Girard Avenue,
Philadelphia,
PA 19104,
U.S.A.

Or, if you live in Canada, to our other sister organization, Wildlife Preservation Trust Canada, at:

17 Isabella Street,
Toronto,
Ontario,
Canada M4Y 1M7.

For most of the species that we deal with time is very short indeed, and we need all the help we can get.

Index